40 ESSENTIAL LIFE SKILLS FOR COLLEGE-AGED YOUNG ADULTS

THE A-Z GUIDE FOR SKILLS EVERY COLLEGE-AGED YOUNG ADULT MUST KNOW

RACHEL LONDON

ROSA REESE

40 Essential Life Skills for College-Aged Young Adults

The A-Z Guide for Skills Every College-Aged Young Adult Must Know

Rachel London

Table of Contents

Table of Contents

❋ Created with Vellum

INTRODUCTION

> You're off to great places! Today is your day!
> So......get on your way!

— DR. SEUSS

Each part of education is a stepping stone for the next part of education. From kindergarten to elementary school, middle school to high school, from college to life; each part builds your academic career, eventually catapulting you (or sinking you) into adulthood and LIFE. Who you become in the world in regard to your occupation is determined by these formative years. However, at some point during these years, you become an adult. Adulting is an interesting concept because even though you have just gone through years of education, no one teaches you to be an adult. Even the most educated people on the planet have to know basic life skills that are not taught in school.

If you got a penny every time someone wished they had a hand-book for life, you'd have more than you could fit in a 55-gallon drum. This is enough pennies to warrant a course of action. Somewhere in this vast world, there will always be someone who feels like they don't know the ins and outs of life, and many people wish for a starting point to work from, at the very least. Life is a rollercoaster that decides to change its twists and turns as it sees fit, and it doesn't give two "cents" about your opinion. In fact, it laughs at your unsuspecting self, throwing in a curve ball or two just for "cents" and giggles.

Sure, life seems easy enough to navigate, especially college. And it feels like that, too, sometimes, when life gives you no other challenges besides who can drink the most shots or date the most. But with all the added stress of taking care of yourself, finding a job, taking care of rent, groceries, mortgage, bank accounts, taxes, etc., it can be a great help to have something to fall back on for a bit of guidance. Only some have it all figured out as soon as they enter the adult world, and most will feel like they have it all together for a short time. I can only describe the feeling as being like a toddler. You stumble, fall, don't know what to say and when to say it, and don't know how anything works; you are practically a baby in the world of adults. That's okay because it will improve with some planning and guidance.

But with all the bumps in the road, it's essential to have some "study material" to refer back to when things get complicated, something you can use to gain more knowledge on a specific topic or how to do something as significant as building a credit score, opening a bank account, applying for college classes, memorizing your social security number, etc. These things might seem simple enough, but without the proper guidance or at least an idea of what to expect, it can become quite challenging—because there is always something else to do, something that seems to trump these things.

According to every feel-good movie that centers around students, you will have nothing to worry about besides beer pong, dating, and your schoolwork (sometimes). Well, if that is your whole idea about college life, you are unfortunately in for a rude awakening as soon as you exceed that threshold. You need to be able to navigate life as if you're a pro because the toddler train is quickly leaving the station.

This book might not get you everything you want in life, and it won't do the work for you, but it will set you up on the right path toward working for it. So buckle up; it's about to get wild.

THE GENERAL ASSORTMENT OF SKILLS

> Create the highest, grandest vision possible for your life, because you become what you believe.

— OPRAH WINFREY

At every stage of your life, there will be a new set of skills being introduced to you. When you're a toddler, you learn how to develop your motor skills by playing with Legos, building blocks, and any other general age-appropriate problem-solving task that requires concentration and coordination. When you're in middle school, you are introduced to newer methods to develop more complex skills that will help you to retain the information needed to succeed at a later stage. This continues in high school, where you are prepared for college.

The purpose of learning these skills is to simplify your life at a later stage by making you used to these scenarios before they have even happened to the extent that they will. For example, learning multiplication tables in elementary school helps you do math more easily in later grades. It also helps you to think in new and evolved ways and helps you to make decisions or solve problems that might have been difficult in the past. Life skills show you a new way of reflecting on the things around you, which helps you build confidence because every "easy" decision and problem you solve helps you build more confidence with every event.

*I*n college, it's important to focus on learning essential skills needed to thrive after school when the real world peeks around the corner and tries to catch you unawares. These skills include time management, managing your goals and planning to reach them, project management, and managing all aspects of your personal life.

As for your career, you can always add a few extra skills to your list. It can significantly improve your chances of landing a job, and even more so, it can improve your chances of becoming successful in the said job within an acceptable amount of time. There is only so much that school books can teach you, but there is no better lesson or teacher than life itself.

MEMORIZING ALL OF THE ESSENTIALS

As a young adult, you'll be given close to a hundred different numbers to memorize. From your social security, student ID, card numbers, phone numbers, and everything else—it can naturally get tricky knowing which is which and remembering it all. Sure, you can carry around a list of numbers, but it's better to know them by heart, just in case.

SOCIAL SECURITY NUMBER

In the United States, a social security number is a nine-digit number issued to U.S. citizens, permanent residents, and temporary residents. The purpose of a social security number is for the government to be able to track you for tax purposes. A social security number may be obtained by filing a form with the US Social Security Administration. This application is usually included with your birth certificate information, and your parents fill this out at the hospital when you are born. A social security card is issued, and your parents typically have it in a safe location, but it is probably time for you to take possession of it. If the card is lost you can contact the Social Security Office or visit their website at www.ssa.gov/ssnumber.

You can also find your social security number on your tax returns, any financial bank statements, or a W-2 or 1099 form. Memorizing your social security number is essential because it lowers the need for you to carry the card around, thus allowing you to keep it in a safe place with other necessary documents.

Knowing the information by heart will help you to apply for a replacement, should your card get lost in the first place. It's also important to remember that keeping this information private and safe is a MUST.

HOW TO KEEP YOUR SOCIAL SECURITY NUMBER SAFE

- Keep the card away in a safe place, preferably among other important papers like your birth certificate, awards, other academic certificates, etc. Keeping everything in the same place helps ensure you won't misplace an important document. Consider storing these important documents in a fireproof box and make certain that a reliable friend or family member knows where it is in case of an emergency.

Example Social Security Card

- Never share your social security number with anyone who calls and asks for it—no company will ever require you to share sensitive information like that with them, not your bank, phone service, or any other subscriptions you have. Nine out of ten times, it's a scam. You cannot give them even five of your social security number; this puts your privacy and safety at risk. Not in the sense that the SWAT team or an assassin will be coming after you, at least.

- Be wary of whom you share the last four numbers of your social security number with. These four numbers are uniquely yours, as each person has a unique combination of the last four. Scammers can quickly figure out the rest of the numbers but not so quickly the last four. Be careful.
- If a service provider or bank contacts you regarding your social security, don't hesitate to ask questions. If you're a non-confrontational or introvert, you probably just went white as a sheet at that. But you must gather as much information as possible before giving them personal information—to ensure your privacy and safety. If a question is nagging in your head, ask it. It can be as innocent as, "What will you use this information for?" Sometimes, they'll offer you the information right off the bat, but if not, don't be shy to ask as many questions as you want until you're comfortable.

APPLYING FOR A REPLACEMENT

You are allowed three replacements within one year (on certain occasions) and ten for your lifetime. Your replacements are free, but that doesn't mean you get to be "loose" with your social security card. Requesting another social security card would look something like this:

- You have to be a US citizen above the age of 18.
- You can only request a replacement if you are not looking to change any information on the new one, like your name, surname, etc.
- You have to have a driver's license or an ID Card.

- You can apply for a replacement card with all these requirements.
- On the other hand, if you are one of the unfortunate few to have your social security stolen, you can follow the steps below to secure your safety and possibly request a replacement.
- In this situation, you must first alert the Social Security Administration—whether it was stolen, lost, or used to commit fraud. Notify them as soon as you find out.
- Make sure to keep an eye on your credit in the near future. Trust me. You don't want to carry the burden of someone else's scams.
- File a police report immediately.
- You should receive an annual report from the social security office regarding how much you pay into the service. Examine this closely for any odd amounts or unexpected payments, as someone else could be using your social security number.

CREDIT CARD NUMBERS

Your credit card will contain the following information:

- your bank
- a number that is unique to your card
- your name
- the expiration date of the card
- your payment network logo
- 3-digit security code on the back

Your credit card number will consist of fifteen numbers, the first six being the IIN (Issuer Identification Number) or BIN (Bank Identification Number). These digits are for the identification of your financial institution, and the first number in the combination is the MII (Major Industry Identifier), which the American Banking Association allots. American Express cards usually begin with 3, Visa cards begin with 4, Discover cards begin with 6, and Mastercards usually begin with 5. The last five digits of your credit card number will indicate or represent the specific bank that issued you the card. They initiate the information for a transaction to occur.

Your account number will be a series of numbers right after the IIN. There are usually, at most, six numbers as a standard, but it can go up to twelve numbers occasionally. This number is unique to you and assigned by the bank to each individual.

TOP TIPS YOU NEED TO KNOW BEFORE YOU USE A CREDIT CARD

A credit card is not simply a means of access to "free money." Think of it more as a loan than a golden opportunity to purchase that shiny new pair of boots or those new Nikes you saw in the store window. In that sense, you are not using what you consider "your money." You are instead using the credit card issuer's money with the unspoken commitment and promise of paying back the loan. Every loan has a set bill date, and you will be charged interest for every missed bill due date—

of course, this is only applicable if you have received a loan. Please note that the interest rates for credit cards might not seem a lot at first, but they can snowball very quickly, and soon you could be required to sacrifice other financial responsibilities and goals to compensate for this one.

YOUR CREDIT SCORE

This is where life, or society, has decided to throw you a curveball. Your credit score is the one thing that could complicate or simplify your life if you know how to be responsible with your credit card. In some states, a too-low credit score can impact your mortgage and car loans, but an absurdly high credit score can do the same. Complete books are written on strategies to build and maintain a good credit score. My goal is to educate you on the utmost importance of this number, but first, I want to give you a quick summary of credit scores and how they work.

A credit score is a three-digit number that ranges from 300-850, and this number estimates how good you are at paying back your bills. The higher the score, the better the person is at paying bills and having the ability to pay back the money they borrow. Credit scores are calculated by gathering information about your credit accounts. There are credit bureaus, or agencies, that collect this information. The three primary credit bureaus are Equifax, Experian, and TransUnion. Now, other companies get this information from the credit bureaus and convert all of this information into a three-digit number called your credit score.

The two primary companies that issue these numbers are FICO and VantageScore (with FICO being the predominant one). This three-digit number (again, from 350-800) gives an estimate of the borrower's creditworthiness. Banks and lenders use this information to determine how much money to lend an individual and how much interest they will charge you. Although ranges vary depending on the agency used, general credit scores are summarized below:

- BAD - 300 to 579
- FAIR - 580 to 669
- GOOD - 670 to 739
- VERY GOOD - 740 to 799
- EXCELLENT - 800 to 850

In many cases, getting your first credit card is the starting point for building your credit score. Being responsible with your credit card is of the utmost importance. You cannot afford to spend above a certain amount, preferably an amount you can pay back—comfortably. Your credit card can be the best way to build up a good credit score, but it can ruin it just as fast. Your credit card issuer reports your habits—how much you borrow when you pay it back, or if you even pay—to the credit bureaus. Your habits, along with the following, are what mainly affect your credit score:

Your payment history—how often you pay, whether you pay on time, etc. This counts for at least 35% of your credit score, and it can be boosted by your payment history if you have responsible habits (D. Schwartz, 2022).

How much of your available credit is being used? This makes up 30% of your score (D. Schwartz, 2022). However, taking up more than half of your limit can cause your score to lower. In other words, using your credit card sparingly or excessively can be the opposite of what you want. But by using it enough to keep your percentage at 30%, you'll generally achieve a good credit score.

CAN I GET A CREDIT CARD AS A STUDENT?

You'll have to meet a list of requirements before being eligible for a credit card. You have to earn adequate money to support the costs in the first place, and you have to have a job—whether it be part-time or full-time. Other ways to acquire a credit card without having to work part-time:

Having your parents or guardian co-sign on your card means that whatever debt you make will also fall on them, which means that you must always stay on top of your payments.

Your parent or guardian could add you as an authorized user, which is mutually beneficial—as you get the benefit of their credit habits, you get to build credit, and you don't have to have your card to do that. Your parents can monitor your spending habits and teach you responsibility in a controlled environment. Although, you will be responsible for their debt if they don't make their payments promptly.

BEFORE YOU GET A CREDIT CARD

While the above might suggest that it's relatively easy to apply for a credit card, some aspects/factors still need to be considered before you attempt to do anything.

Make sure you know how to budget efficiently. You need to be able to keep track of your spending and the amount of money you're receiving to make sure that there is always a balance between your income/allowance and your spending—to ensure that you don't unintentionally ruin your credit score before you've had a chance even to build one. This skill will also help you to plan for more serious stuff like paying bills, paying your student loans, buying groceries, etc. Financial literacy and budgeting are of the utmost importance and something you should consider improving before getting a credit card.

You have to have an existing bank account. If you don't already have a bank account, you must open one before applying for a credit card. You will ideally need a savings account to deposit any extra money you have and want to save. And you'll also need a checking account; both will need to be checked daily to ensure you're keeping track of your money.

Start slow with a debit card. With a debit card, you can make mistakes without having too dire consequences. If you spend too much money through your debit account, many times, banks will pay this for you, but they charge you an "overdraft fee," which usually ranges from $30 to $50 per transaction. This does not affect your credit score but can get expensive quickly. This allows you some wiggle room, if you will. Because a debit card doesn't deal with any loans but rather with the actual balance in your bank account. Therefore, you won't accidentally be able to ruin your credit score by making a few questionable purchases; it just might get really expensive. Think of it as a 'free pass' to make a few mistakes at just the cost of a few bucks instead of at the cost of a bad credit score. Always check with your bank to see if your account is eligible for overdraft protection and to see how much this costs per transaction.

MEMORIZING YOUR CARD DETAILS

As mentioned, memorizing your credit card details is only in your best interest. There will be instances where you'll need the information but won't have your card, which will be a lifesaver. One especially effective method for memorization is the Major method.

THE MAJOR METHOD

This is a technique that makes use of number combinations and links those numbers to letter combinations similar in form or sound. This method is effective because it uses a few techniques to link numbers like those on your credit card and convert them into letters. This is especially helpful if you're more of a literary than a math-oriented person—because not everyone's memory is the same, in the sense that nobody's brains work the same. The steps to utilizing this method:

Every number from 0-9 represents a consonant—in other words, every letter except the vowels a, e, i, o, u, and y.

You'll start by finding similarities between some letters and a number. For example, a 3 turned upside down resembles the letter "M." The number 2 turned on its side looks like an "N." Get it? Every number will have its own set of letters that can be used to remember it. 0 is "Z" because of Zero or "S" because of a soft "C" sound—like "zero" or "cero."

This is effective because you can form words and make visual examples of the numbers on the card. For example, if you take 2993—it would "translate" into NOOB. The 2 beings "N," the double 9 is the two "O"s, and the 3 is the "B."

You can do this with every combination of four letters—as is the standard on all cards, especially for better memorization—and flip them into images.

BE WARY OF SCAMMERS

Unfortunately, money is the axis the world turns on because you can do nothing without it besides breathing. You have to have money to eat, you have to have money to live in a home, you have to have money to get an education, and you have to have money for something as basic as using the bathroom—paying for water, toilet paper, etc. Therefore, people can get inventive when accumulating money—very inventive and sneaky. You must protect critical information, such as your credit card number.

Because of the beautiful and advancing age of technology, you no longer need a physical card to be able to commit credit card fraud. All you need are a few essential digits and a name, and you're set. And I know you're wondering how they might get the number in the first place, and, unfortunately, it's pretty easy.

Not long ago, I received an email telling me I needed to update the information on my Google account. I quickly googled the link, immediately realizing it was a scam. Well, I had to shut the account entirely down because the scammer somehow jumbled up all my emails, and I could no longer access what I needed to access. There are so many ways hackers can get your information. Below is a summary of some of these.

How Fraudsters Steal Your Credit Card Information

- hacking into payment portals of online stores
- stealing your info via "shoulder-surfing" while at ATMs, registers, etc.
- scam phone calls and posing as your bank or service provider—some of them even go as far as calling to confirm a fake purchase
- stealing your wallet or picking up lost cards
- scouting for discarded credit cards in dumpsters
- stealing your information via a Wi-Fi network
- intercepting contactless payment portals—the "tap" feature that has become so popular now (or Venmo, PayPal, etc.)
- making use of spyware on devices

- hacking websites you trust to access payment portals
- hacking your bank account—not as expected, but it happens
- fake emails and "prizes" that you won
- fake texts or instant messages

These are used more frequently because they most effectively steal someone's information. Most people fall for the ruse and click on the attached links, giving the hackers access to your phone—and everything else.

HOW TO PROTECT YOUR INFORMATION

These are some preventative measures you can incorporate to make sure you don't fall prey to the fraudsters out there:

Keep your card close when purchasing in a store and shield your information from shoulder surfers.

Try your best not to pay with credit online or over the phone. This limits your chances of getting scammed. Also, remember that any financial institution or service provider will never ask for your card number or card details.

Keep track of your credit, and continually monitor your bank statements and any incoming or outgoing money.

Make use of a credit freeze. This is when you contact the credit bureau and ask them not to let anyone pull your credit information until you "unfreeze" this, which is done by emailing them.

Set limits on your credit cards. Let's say you have a limit on your credit card of $10,000. You can tell the credit card company that you only want access to $3,000 of this money unless you specifically notify them. This prevents thieves from spending above a certain amount, which protects your credit history.

Permanently remove your cards from websites, and never save any passwords or cards online.

Make sure you're on a safe site before entering any card details. You can look for confirmation of this by looking for a green lock next to the site address. Or you can see if it there is an 's' right after the http://. The safer site will look like this: https://. HTTPS is more secure than HTTP because it uses encryption protection information between clients and servers.

THE WARNING SIGNS

There are always warning signs regarding credit card fraud, especially if you're suspicious of activity on your account. Here are signs to watch out for:

- any unconfirmed, suspicious, or large purchases that you did not make yourself
- if your bank sends an alert of suspicious activity
- if there are large sums of money being withdrawn from your account or spent online

STUDENT ID

Your student ID is one of the most important things you own while in college. But it's also the thing you'll most likely misplace or lose. Memorization is great for those days when you overslept and forgot your student ID but desperately need it.

MNEMONIC MEMORY

This term is used to define the act of using mnemonics to make connections between something we vaguely remember and something we know well. These mnemonic devices are used to remember new information and can be made use of audibly/verbally, auditory, or via acoustic cues based on previously retained information.

People who use mnemonic devices can memorize large amounts of information more quickly and recall the information faster. This is an efficient memorization method because many techniques best suit your learning ability.

GROUP NUMBERS

It always works better to memorize a number when grouped into four or five chunks rather than an unending string. Think about when you memorized your parents' numbers, addresses, etc.

Breaking the extensive string of numbers into chunks will help you memorize them in combinations rather than this one big string with no beginning or end. It's easier to recall the numbers, and you won't be mixing them up as much. Try for groups of three to four; if you're really good, you can try for five.

THROUGH SONG

Do you know how people profess their love through song? Well, it's worth more than telling the girl or guy how much you love them. You can use a ringtone or melody to remember information. Have you noticed that you remember every lyric to your favorite songs? Well, connecting information and concepts to songs will work similarly. You'll have no trouble recalling the information precisely.

MAKE USE OF ACRONYMS

Breaking the information down into acronyms will make retaining large amounts more accessible than memorizing it word for word. You can break the information into smaller sections, which aids in memory retention.

You can decide which devices/methods will best help you memorize your student ID. It's all about what works for you and how it benefits you. You are unique; therefore, you need to adapt to your surroundings.

MAKE USE OF AN APP

If you have trouble with memorization, as I have had in the past, you might not even want to attempt those mentioned above—which is okay. Using an app is expected today and relatively easy, considering how many different apps exist. One of the keys to using an app is to have a rock-solid password. You must memorize this because if you have all your essential passwords in this "vault," security must be paramount. So, here are some apps you could use to help you remember all of your passwords and pins and numbers while keeping them safe:

- LastPass
- Dashlane
- Bitwarden
- Enpass
- Keeper
- Nordpass
- Zoho Vault

PROJECT AND GOAL MANAGEMENT

Goals are the ultimate result that you are trying to achieve. This result comprises different milestones that will propel you forward and closer to achieving all of your goals—short-term or long-term. They keep you going, motivate you, and help you make decisions that will positively affect your future.

Sure, the milestones can be challenging and might not always work out. But that's why it's essential to start from the beginning. You need to know how to set goals and milestones before you can work to achieve them. And you're wondering how difficult it can be to set a milestone because it seems relatively straightforward. But it's all about setting achievable and perceivable goals.

MILESTONES

A milestone is a unique or significant position of change or growth. And the significance of your development or growth can only be defined by you. You can measure your milestone's significance by considering your main goal. For example, if you're trying to learn how to cook, then making an egg omelet can be considered a milestone, especially if you couldn't even make scrambled eggs before. This is significant because you have gone from a starting point (which is your inability to make scrambled eggs) and progressed to a milestone (being able to make an omelet) that will set you on track to achieve your goal (being able to cook). Make sense? Yes.

SETTING MILESTONES

SET YOUR END GOAL

Chances are you already know your end goal, whether short term, like acing next week's test, or long term, like graduating college in a few years. But goals can entail personal, financial, spiritual, social, and work.

SET YOUR STARTING POINT

This is where self-awareness and honesty come in. You must be 'real' about where you're starting from. For example, your goal is to ace the test next week. You know you haven't studied one bit and don't know anything about the subject you're writing the test about. But you can't be honest enough to set realistic milestones. So you decide to start from the middle of your study material instead of at the start. This causes you to score lower on your test than you thought. You can see how a real starting point is essential. A realistic and honest starting point is the best way to determine achievable milestones.

USE THE SMART METHOD TO SET YOUR MILESTONES

Once a starting point and an end goal have been established, you need to focus on the milestones to help you achieve that goal. The SMART goal method is excellent for setting measurable and achievable milestones. SMART is an acronym for:

- Specific
- Measurable
- Achievable
- Relevant
- Time-Bound

SPECIFIC

Be detailed in your description of the goal/milestone you are setting. For example, you must set a specific percentage or goal to improve your grades. Do you want to improve all of your grades by a certain percentage? Do you want your GPA to be a certain number? Do you want to achieve a particular grade for each of your subjects? Your milestones need to be specific to know how to achieve them.

MEASURABLE

Your milestones must be measurable in order for you to be able to track your progress and stay motivated. A measurable goal is a goal that has specific, measurable numbers. For example, my goal in my World Civilization class will be to get a 93 or an A- on my subsequent examination. Or my goal for my next physics test is to increase my grade by ten points over the last test. Another example would be that I want to be able to run a 5K race, without stopping, in the next six weeks. By making your goals measurable, you are making yourself accountable to yourself.

ACHIEVABLE

Your goals have to be achievable by nature. If you set goals or milestones that seem impossible and are basically impossible for where you are in life at this moment, it can have a really negative effect on your confidence and your motivation. For example, you are a beginner runner and aim to run 125 miles nonstop by the end of the month. It is unachievable, not only because you're a beginner but also because it is impossible for the best runners. Setting unachievable goals will have a negative effect on your motivation and your confidence. You will feel inadequate or like a failure because you didn't achieve that goal, and you might not want to keep exercising if you believe it's all for nothing.

Instead, weigh your starting point with your end goal and define a measurable milestone—like a whopping 11 miles when you're a seasoned runner and 1 mile when you're just starting. Those are both achievable and measurable. You'll feel accomplished and motivated when you accomplish that goal, maybe more than ever. As mentioned above, you need to be able to realistically achieve your goals for them to be goals in the first place. If you're counting on a miracle to make them happen, they move out of the goal category into the dream category. The difference between a desire and a goal is that a goal can be accomplished with effort.

RELEVANT

Your milestones must be relevant to the overall achievement of your main goal. Using the same example as before, if your goal is to run 10 miles comfortably, you will start small and keep increasing your distance as you go along to achieve the main goal—being able to run 10 miles comfortably. Whatever will contribute to your success and achievement or the development of your goal is what you would call a relevant milestone.

TIME-BOUND

Set a specific and achievable time frame or due date for your milestone. That test you want to ace? It is due next week, so you should set your studying milestones at least a day or two before that. For example, if you write on Monday, you should set your milestone to finish studying by Saturday at least. Time constraints on milestones will keep you motivated and add the little bit of healthy pressure you need to get it done.

SUMMARY

So, using the SMART method is a way to hold yourself accountable because you clearly know what your goals are. You can monitor your progress, or lack thereof, at all times.

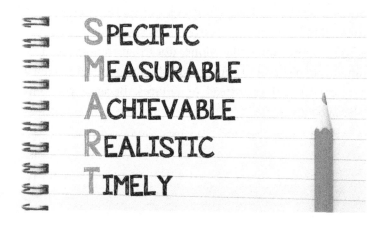

JOT IT DOWN

Writing down your milestones will help you elaborate further on them and define what they mean to you and their significance for your main goal. According to research, your chances of actually accomplishing that goal improve by 42% when the goal is written down (Hall, Lifehack, 2021). Visualization is absolutely critical for perseverance. Having a calendar or some other method of showing each goal helps you see when milestones are reached. Seeing your progress helps you keep the goal in view.

DON'T BE TOO HARD ON YOURSELF

As with life, not everything you want to do will happen as you wanted it to or as you pictured it. Sometimes, when life is ruthless, it will prevent you from achieving some of your goals entirely. And I'm here to tell you it's okay if you don't achieve all of them. Thomas Edison once said, "I have not failed. I've just found 10,000 ways that won't work.....Our greatest weakness lies in giving up. The most certain way to succeed is always to try just one more time."

But you need to realize that it's okay, too. Don't be too hard on yourself for not accomplishing things you thought you would— because more times than none, does that "failure" lead you to something bigger and better? Adjust your mindset to view these moments as delays instead of failures. Because you only fail when you give up.

USING A TIMETABLE TO ORGANIZE YOUR PROJECTS AND GOALS

Using a timetable to promote better time management is a big step in the right direction. You must manage your time better to ensure enough time to do everything needed.

Good time management ensures less procrastination that you're meeting your deadlines on time, and it helps you to not stress so much—because everything is in order like it should be.

PRIORITIZE YOUR GOALS AND PROJECTS

Time management is vital to being organized and getting things done on time. It will help you to balance your social life and your academics while in college, and it will help you to juggle your career, personal life, and everything else when you've graduated. It is an essential skill that has nothing but beneficial consequences.

When sketching a timetable, the first order of business is to prioritize your goals and projects from important to least important. Be honest with yourself and make sure you're prioritizing correctly; otherwise, this exercise is all for naught. For example:

Project/Activity	Due Date
English paper	February 15
History test	February 27
Job interview	March 15

Project Chart

*A*s you can see from the table above, I've prioritized my projects and goals according to the dates they are due —which links to their importance. I won't prepare for my test as much this week because I need to spend most of my time on my English paper. Always arrange your priorities according to their importance and due date. This will improve your time management and planning, ensuring no late hand-ins, all your projects get done on time, and significantly lowering your stress. Now that you have prioritized your month, further break this down into weekly "chunks," so you have monthly, weekly, and daily plans. Again, use the SMART method for these projects and goals.

REMEMBER TO TAKE NEEDED BREAKS

If you're working yourself to death without making time for breaks or a moment to catch your breath, you'll get so burned out and end up not doing as well as you wanted.

It's vital for your health to take breaks in between these draining activities and projects. Refueling your mind and allowing it to take a breather will only help you in the long run —plus, you get to scrape up some motivation to do it all again.

CONCENTRATED TIME

Multiple studies have shown that concentrated study time is much more efficient, effective, and productive than distracted study time. This means you must deliberately take distractions out of the equation to boost your productivity. Unfortunately, that means we have to turn off our cell phones, postpone reading emails, listening to voicemails, and reading laptop notifications. When studying, turn your phone to silent for a specified time. You can even set your timer for thirty to forty-five minutes and then give yourself a ten-minute break. You will be shocked at how much more productive and effective you will be by having this full time.

2

I'M CATCHING THE RED EYE - TRAVEL AND FASHION

> Better to see something once than to hear about it a thousand times.
>
> — ASIAN PROVERB

You're young and want to be out on the town, making memories, making questionable decisions, and enjoying your youth—as you should. But the only problem you face with the above is that you're in desperate need of transportation to get to said "memory making." This section will tell you all there is to know about public transportation and tips on making it the best experience. Because let's face it, some questionable characters sometimes take the bus or train. You might say this does not pertain to me because I live in a small town. Take my advice; you never know where you will be tomorrow, next week, or next year. And we all like to travel.

THE YELLOW CAR VERSUS THE APP

This is a time in your life when moving around town is a priority. You may have your own vehicle, but sometimes it is hard to access your car, or you want to keep your parking spot. Let's face it, there also be times that you should not be driving, such as after a party or a big game. Whatever the reason may be, hiring a driver will be something that you will need to be able to do.

One of the most convenient, efficient, and fastest modes of transportation is hailing a taxi. In big cities, you can walk up to an intersection and look around for taxis, hold your thumb up, and you will be picked up in record-breaking time. When getting in the taxi, you tell the driver where you want to go, they drive to that destination, and you pay them what they tell you it will cost after your arrival. Taxi services cost a premium, but the convenience can be nice. Ten years ago, the only way to travel without your own vehicle was to use the taxi service, but now you have options.

Ride-share apps like Uber, Lyft, and Grab have now given us other options when it comes to hiring a driver, and to be honest, they have completely changed how people travel in cities. Ride-share apps are usually better than using a taxi. Your location geographically will determine which ride-share app will be the best. Most apps are easy to use, less expensive, safer (maybe not perfect), and more convenient than taxis. Advantages of ride-sharing apps include:

- Convenience - You can order your driver on your phone, confirm the cost, schedule ahead of time, pay by credit card (already saved in your phone), and even vet the drivers.

- No haggling over price - You can clearly see the prices and decide which service you want to order directly over your phone.
- Safety - Ride-share apps implement a review system for all of their drivers. This allows the user to view the driver's rating, and you can set a minimum number of star ratings in your phone so that you only accept drivers who have met your criteria.
- GPS Monitoring - When using the apps, you can monitor the route you are traveling with a built-in GPS mapping system. Some apps even allow you to "share your ride" with family or friends in real-time, thereby increasing the safety factor.
- Options - When using the app, you can order a compact car, medium size car, or even a minibus, depending on your needs.

These ride-sharing apps have many benefits, but they are not always the best option. Lots of factors can negate the benefits of these ride-sharing apps. Availability, length of the ride, time of day, and geographic availability can change the price and options of these ride services, so you have to review all of the options. Now, let's discuss other modes of transportation.

THE BUS

The bus is one of the cheapest ways to get to and from, especially when traveling a considerable distance. And booking a bus ticket is super simple, even though it might sound daunting.

- You'll start by entering your city's name and information regarding a bus pass.
- Then you simply follow the on-screen instructions until your ticket is booked.

- You'll need to plan your trip,
- Every bus follows a specific route and doesn't usually veer off it.
- The buses will be marked with specific numbers that indicate which route they will be taking—this information can be found at your local central bus station.
- Select which route you want to take using the maps provided by your bus station online. If you can't find the correct route, you can go to the central station and ask for assistance from the information desk.
- Ensure you're familiar with the bus schedule—where it stops, when, and if it works on the days you plan to take the bus—just to ensure you're not stranded.
- On your journey, make sure to be at your bus stop on time, every time. If you're going to take the bus a lot, it might be cheaper to buy a monthly bus pass. Please remember that when taking the bus, you will need the exact change it will cost—bus drivers don't usually carry change.

BUS PAYMENT

Well, this section depends on which of the options you'll choose. You have a few:

- You buy a monthly pass.
- You buy a bus pass.
- You pay for every ride in cash.
- You pay with tokens.

Monthly Pass

Bus companies offer many bus pass options. Some are for unlimited access, and some have specifics, like how many rides you can take with a certain pass. Some grant a certain percentage discount—for students or the elderly. Usually, you can buy these passes online or at the bus station.

Pay with Tokens

You can buy bus tokens at a specific price and use them as payment instead of carrying loose change around. You can enquire about them at the bus administrative office or find the information online.

Pay With Cash

You can go the old-fashioned way and pay your fare with cash. Please remember that it is coins only, and you can deposit the payment into a farebox at the front of the bus. You'll also be asked to show your ID, so have that ready.

SUBWAY OR METRO

This section is for you if you prefer the railway over the stuffy bus. And no matter in which city you are, there are a few things that stay the same no matter where you go (in the US, that is):

- You have to get a pass or ticket for the subway.
- You will have more than one platform connecting you to the train—so just take a deep breath when that panic sets in.
- Most subway systems employ an app service for your phone to help in planning, maps, arrival and departing times, station information, and more.
- Tickets are usually bought at the subway station but can be bought directly through the app or online.

- You must use the route map to determine where you must get off—it will be the Sam to your Frodo.
- Every train station has more than two entryways and more than two exit points. You must determine which will work best based on your drop-off location.
- This is very important; the train has AUTOMATIC doors. So please do not stick anything out of the train because you will be caught off guard.

The pros of taking the subway are as follows:

- You get to save money since it's considerably cheaper than private transport.
- It's faster, and you'll get to your destination more promptly.
- There's more space, there's no traffic, and it's better for the environment (which is a huge pro).
- It's a lot safer, considering they have CCTV cameras everywhere.

TRAVELING BY TRAIN

There are some things you'll need to be able to travel via the train:

- your ID
- your ticket
- an ID tag for your baggage

Before you travel anywhere, you must research potential routes you want to take and how you should plan your travel to reach the correct locations. Research railways and routes, and make sure to book ahead of time. The most common passenger train in the United States is Amtrak. Amtrak has a robust website to help you plan your travel route.

How to Book

Please make sure to always book in advance to make sure you have secured a spot for yourself, but as for the type of ticket you need to book;

Premium Fare

In this category, you have another two options; the first-class fare (which Amtrak calls Acela), which includes beverages, food, and special lounges. Or, the Sleeper, where you are given a room and beds to make yourself comfortable for a long or overnight journey.

Flexible Fare

These fares are refundable without having to pay any cancellation fees, as well as elastic reservations. This is very obviously the best method of train travel if you are someone who travels impulsively as opposed to carefully planning. This fare allows you to explore on your way to your destination.

*V*alue Fare

This option is available everywhere but doesn't necessarily have all the refund policies others might have. There is also limited availability regarding seats for this specific fare.

Business Fare

This fare offers an advanced and more comfortable travel experience (way to sound like an ad). These fares also include beverages and a bit more wiggle room.

Saver Fare

This is the fare with the lowest rate and close to none of the perks the other fares have, and they also have the least space— which is precisely why booking in advance is so important.

TRAVEL BY FLIGHT

This section is essential unless you plan to sprout wings and do it yourself. Especially if you travel frequently, or rather, plan to. Even if you do not plan to be a work traveler, chances are that you will have to travel by plane sometime in the next ten years, so pay close attention to this section.

BOOKING A TICKET

FLIGHT SEARCH

If you book your ticket via the airline's website, the website will send your request directly to the airline, showing you a list of available flights from that airline.

Another method to book a ticket is to use a third-party website that will allow you to compare prices, flight times, seats, etc., between different airlines. This is useful if you are one of the people who like to compare services before making a decision.

BOOKING

It's easier if your book seats directly with the airline because it will simplify the cancellation (should something happen). I like to do a Google search for plane tickets from and to with the exact dates. For example, I use a Google search to go from Denver on June 1 to Nashville and returned to Denver on June 7. Then I look at one of the many third-party websites to see my airline offers and flight options. This is a quick way to see the approximate prices and times available. Then, I go directly to the specific airline's website. You will also get a wider variety to choose from if you are booking directly with the airline as opposed to a third party.

Additionally, the airline must check the availability of the seats you want to book—so it will be easier for them to pinpoint. If your seats are available, the screen will show you an "HK" indicating your "Holding Confirmed." If you receive a "UN," the carrier cannot approve the request.

ANCILLARY BOOKING

This is a fancy term for referring to all the "extras" you might want to add to your flight. For example, you have SSR (Special Service Request) codes that you can add, which the airline will then change using your PNR number. PNR is the abbreviation for Passenger Name Record. This is a type of digital certificate that allows passengers to do online check-ins and just to overall manage their bookings. Here are some of the other codes.

- EXST—an extra seat.
- KSML—a kosher meal.
- LSML—a meal with low salt.
- PETC—for animals, such as service dogs, etc.
- Check-In, Boarding, and Everything Else

You have a few options when it comes to check-in, and thanks to technology, the whole process has been simplified—significantly so, might I add—in the last few years. If you know what you're doing, you could be "in and out" before breaking a sweat.

ONLINE

You can usually check in online 24-48 hours before your flight because that's the only time the window is available—unless the airline has its specific "rules" surrounding this. You will simply have to enter your ticket information into the website, which will have access to a seating chart that you can choose from. If you don't choose a specific seat, you'll be assigned one automatically, along with your boarding pass. Most airlines also offer an app for your phone, which is often a convenient way to check-in.

AIRPORT

Alternatively to doing a complete online check-in, you can just check in at the airport. At the check-in counter, you'll present your e-ticket to the agent to have them enter the details into the system. You will be given a boarding pass to be presented to the agent at your gate.

BAGGAGE CLAIM

Your baggage will be assigned a ten-digit code or barcode to track it properly. This is how airlines prevent your luggage from getting lost and are also used by the airport's system to sort the baggage accordingly—the system scans the barcodes.

EVERYTHING YOU CAN'T TAKE

If you think you're sly enough to sneak some of your things onto the airplanes—things you know are not allowed, besides the illegal stuff—then you are delusional. However, if you are genuinely unaware of the do's and don'ts of hand luggage, look no further.

DO'S WHEN FLYING

You are allowed to bring small tools on board. This encompasses all tools besides small screwdrivers, wrenches, pliers, and anything smaller than 7 inches. You can also bring nail clippers, small scissors (no longer than 4 inches), and pill cutters. The rest are a definite no-go.

Any liquids less than 3.4 ounces and non-flammable are allowed on the plane. This includes any toiletries, aerosols, or gels that meet the above requirements.

Lighters and matches (believe it or not) are also allowed on board. Standard book matches and a normal lighter are allowed. However, you are prohibited from carrying any 'strike-anywhere' matches. You must carry these items in your carry-on luggage, as they cannot be stashed in check-in luggage.

You can carry any AA, AAA, D, and C batteries on board—in either your carry-on or checked luggage. However, loose lithium batteries must be stowed in your carry-on as they are not permitted in checked.

Knitting needles are also permitted, provided they are thoroughly wrapped to prevent any injury or punctures in your luggage.

Wrapped gifts are also allowed if they meet the safety and security requirements. It might be wiser to leave the gifts unwrapped because security screeners tend to unwrap them for inspection.

Medication and specific medical equipment are permitted on board, but only if the medication is available over the counter or prescribed, and other necessities like inhalers, EpiPens, casts, blood-sugar tester kits, etc. You are not limited to the previously mentioned, but any medical necessities must be reported to the security screeners before boarding.

Electronic cigarettes, vapes, and everything else that puffs. You can carry your 'smoking device' on board, provided the liquid is below the 3.4-ounce cutoff. The liquid must be checked at the security screenings if it is more than that. Battery-powered devices can only be brought on board in your carry-on or person.

Electric and disposable razors are allowed on board.

DON'TS WHEN FLYING

Any sharp objects (besides the exceptions mentioned earlier) like box cutters, knives (very obviously, might I add), meat cleavers—honestly, this should also be a given—and any other sharp objects that can be used to intentionally or unintentionally injure someone. But as mentioned before, if you have permitted sharp objects such as small scissors, they must be wrapped as a precaution.

Sports equipment is not allowed on the plane as carry-ons. Any sports-related equipment, such as hockey sticks, baseball bats, etc., should be checked in with the rest of your luggage.

Self-defense sprays, weapons, and other items are not allowed on board and will not pass security.

Large amounts of alcohol, and beverages with an alcohol percentage above 70%, cannot be taken on board or checked in. But if you want to bring wine or champagne home as a gift, you must know that you can carry up to five liters in your baggage. These may be more than 24% alcohol but less than 70%. Your beverages must be unopened and sealed in their original unopened retail packaging.

DRESS CODE FOR FLYING AND TRAVEL

When traveling, I think it is important to find the best mixture of comfort and class. Don't get me wrong, I enjoy dressing down and being comfortable just as much as the next person, but when traveling, I like to lean towards the side of classy and put-together. My rule of thumb is to never wear anything that you would feel embarrassed or ashamed if you were to run into your preacher, your boss, or your ex-boyfriend or girlfriend. No matter if it is fair or not, you are generally treated better if you look the part, so you need to take accountability for how you present yourself (whether you are jet-setting in a private jet or taking an Uber to lunch).

Of course, comfort is also important when you have a six-hour flight and you are cramped into a small window seat next to an overweight person for the entire time. The great news is that there are great options that can fit the label of class and comfort. My personal go-to is fashionable black leggings, a stylish cotton tee shirt, a light jacket or sweater (even in the summer, there are times when airplanes are cool), and fashionable sneakers. For guys, I recommend a button-down, nice jeans, simple sneakers, and a light jacket.

The next thing we need to talk about is planning to dress for where we are going. If our travels are simply taking us to dinner and a movie, we can get by with one outfit, but if we are traveling to a wedding or job interview, this is going to require a totally different wardrobe. A long day of travel usually will necessitate a change of clothes and sometimes a complete do over of showering and "getting ready again". Again, it is all about planning and decisions of the destination.

JOB INTERVIEW - DRESS TO IMPRESS

What you wear is almost always the first impression people get of you. You might be the sweetest person on Earth, unable to hurt a fly, but wearing spikes and studs with all-black and butt-kicking combat boots. Automatically, you will be perceived as some intense person who either does or doesn't sacrifice tiny kittens. The same goes for the opposite. You could be the meanest, most horrible human being, but if you're sporting a fluffy pink wardrobe, you'll likely be perceived as a kindhearted soul out for peace. Unfortunately, that suggests we rely solely on outer appearances for that initial impression, but it's true. Your wear will portray the image you want to send to the world. That's why dressing appropriately for your job or interview is so important.

The basics of dressing for an interview are the same, but we will be going into specifics regarding gender to ensure every one is as prepared as possible. Some things to consider when picking an ideal and appropriate outfit for your interview;

- Consider your role. Before you decide what to wear for your interview, consider the role you are interviewing for. For example, if you're at an interview for a serving job, you might not want to arrive in a suit with neatly polished shoes. You'll feel out of place and slightly uncomfortable. And while you shouldn't dress too casually either, you can opt for a respectful and neat outfit instead of a full suit with a tie.

- Make sure to be appropriate but comfortable. Some interviews can go on for hours, and you don't want to be confined in something uncomfortable for hours. It might distract you, and let's be honest; it sucks to wear uncomfortable clothes.

- You need to own at least a few pieces of professional-looking attire. This is an investment that you'll find yourself always needing. Professional clothes are needed for interviews or jobs at corporate and respectable places of employment. They can also be used for weddings, funerals, seminars, etc. The bottom line is that you'll always find a use for professional attire.

- Always consider wearing accessories that match the atmosphere or nature of the interview. If you're going to an interview at a company that values straight-cut attire with little wiggle room for personalization or "zhuzh," that funky gold cuff or patterned tie might not cut. Most of the time, the flashy accessories should stay at home—or at least until you've got the job and you've been accustomed to their dress code.

- Always wear the correct shoes—formal shoes, please. Do not wear ballet flats or sneakers with your suits and pencil skirts—that should be against the law. It looks horrible.

- Do not wear too much perfume or cologne because too much can quickly become overkill and have the opposite effect of what you intended.
- Ensure your clothes are ironed and neatly tucked in—if your outfit requires it.

First Impressions Matter

FASHION FOR MEN

In this instance, basic is better. There is nothing so infinitely attractive as a man in a suit. Choose a few essential pieces from your wardrobe—or the shop if you're buying a new suit—and dress it up with other elements. You don't want to go too crazy with patterns and crazy ties, but you also don't want to go too basic. There is a fine line between disrespectful and drop-dead gorgeous.

One way to spice your outfit up is to play around with different color combinations. You'll still be basic and respectful but have the extra "zhuzh" of color. For example, instead of going for your simple gray suit and matching tie—why don't you spruce it up with a royal blue vest and matching tie? That breaks up the dull gray, but you're still basic enough to be dressed for any scenario possible.

Here are some tips if you're not sure what to wear to what:

- If you need clarification on whether business casual or business formal is the way to go, you can opt for a simple khaki slack, a matching navy blazer, and a button-up to meet that middle ground. This look is less intimidating and "in your face" than a black or gray suit, and it is a great middle ground between professional and casual.
- A button-down with a sweater over the top is a fool-proof business casual look that "slays" every time. Neutral colors, such as navy, brown, or black, are always the way to go—because these colors match almost everything.
- A navy blue blazer is a staple piece when it comes to business attire for men. This can be worn with a tie or

without and paired with any type of pants: slacks, khakis, jeans, etc.

- Statement ties are a brave choice, but they can be good if you know how to wear them—instead of it wearing them. If you pair statement ties with the right suit, it can elevate your wardrobe.
- The same goes for a bold shirt. Make sure to stay as neutral as possible to prevent any strange looks (not that you should worry what others think—this should only apply to your career). If you want something funky, opt for a more subtle funk, like a striped shirt or fine dots within the neutral color spectrum.

FASHION FOR WOMEN

Dressing fashionably in professional wear is so easy because it looks flawless and elegant every single time—if you know what you're doing, that is. And let's be honest, who doesn't feel powerful in a suit?

- Always try to go for a top/blouse that is appropriate but also comfortable. A button-down is always a good idea, or you can go for a blouse with a blazer—switch the blazer with a high-neck blouse in the summer—or even a sweater (as long as it's professional and won't bug you all day).
- Always wear shoes with a closed toe—no open-toe shoes ever; it just isn't appropriate workplace attire.
- Ensure your skirt (if you wear skirts) is always just above the knee or longer.
- For accessories, try to keep them professional. Don't be too out there with certain accessories—unless your job permits it. Try a subtle gold necklace or a dainty gold bracelet if you're looking for bling.

- A collared shirt with a long sleeve is always the way to go, especially when paired with a pencil skirt or fitted suit pants.
- Chinos are a great option if you're going for business casual because they can be paired with anything, and they don't look as "professional" as black or gray suits. Pair the chinos with a classy button-down, a pretty blouse, or a plain sweater.
- Always wear a heel or something that looks formal enough to fit with the look you're going for—absolutely no flip-flops or sneakers.

3

LUNCHEONS TO DINNER DATES

> Food is dear to everyone's heart, so the golden rule
> of table manners is respect.

— CRISTINA HO

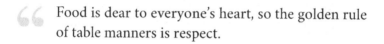eing an adult is knowing the proper etiquette surrounding certain situations. Because believe it or not, adults are seriously bothered by proper etiquette or lack thereof. And it's not just about etiquette; it's about how you are perceived and how well you respect the "rules" of society—for example, tipping. When tipping someone in the service industry, you're walking a tightrope. If you tip but tip too little, you're a stingy good person. But you're the worst person on Earth if you don't tip at all. So, here's a little guide to help you be a decent person with which society can build a relationship.

DINING ETIQUETTE

Have you ever wanted to punch someone slurping hard enough to make you nauseous? Or the person smacking so frequently that your soul seemed to bruise with every wet smack? You've come to the right place if you have felt that burning anger. This is a safe space for people like us.

Some rules need to be followed when dining, especially when dining with other people outside of your inner circle. You want to make a good impression on these people and show them respect. These things are accomplished by having basic table manners and etiquette.

Dining Rules

RESTAURANT ETIQUETTE

The basic rules of dining are as follows:

- Constantly chew with your mouth closed—and don't talk with your mouth full, for that matter.
- Never have your phone on the table. And if it is a must, always have the ringer off.
- Always clean yourself in the privacy of the bathroom—never at the table.
- Don't put your elbows on the table.

- Ask for food or items to be passed to you down the table, do not reach over the table.
- Do not rush your eating.
- Use your napkin, and wipe any food that litters your face.
- Dress nicely if the scene of the restaurant requires it— or if you feel like it, there's no shame in the dressing- nice game.
- Don't yell to get the waiter's attention—that's just rude, in any case.

DINING ETIQUETTE

Always make sure to arrive on time or a little before time for any of your events. It shows class and professionalism; it's for work or an opportunity. Being on time is not only a great first impression on someone but also sets the "date" up on the right foot. Punctuality is key. More tips for proper dining etiquette:

- Do not place bags, keys, or your phone on the table when dining with other people—especially if it's in a formal setting.
- Do not slouch, and keep your elbows from resting on the table.
- Always place your utensils on the plate instead of the table.
- Use your napkin.
- Tear your bread into small pieces; never bite a whole chunk off.
- After eating, place your utensils diagonally on the plate.
- Stir your soup to cool it down instead of blowing on it.

HOW TO ORDER AT A RESTAURANT

To ensure you start the evening or the meal on a good foot, greet your servers before just rattling off your order. A simple "Hi, how are you?" will make your server feel so much better—because some people don't always consider that this is an actual person they're dealing with.

Additionally, consider the kind of restaurant you're at. Is it a bar setting where you order dive food? Is it a fancy restaurant with a white glove service? Is it a fast-food restaurant where speed is valued above all else? This will affect how you order and interact with the staff. For example, yelling and rattling off your order in a bar works better than doing it in a fancy restaurant.

The above should also be considered with your arrival—how you will be greeted and greeted them. At restaurants, especially the fancier ones, you will be addressed formally—like, party of how many? Or a table for two/four/six?—whereas at more informal dining settings like bars or fast food restaurants, it's free for all. There are no reserved seats; you will likely have to swing for a table.

As for the bill, this can be settled in multiple ways. For restaurants, it's usually better to have split bills from the start—if you guys don't plan on 'treating' each other. That avoids the uncomfortable conversation of how much each one of you owes. And it makes for less work for the server—there is nothing worse than having to split a bill after everyone has eaten and you try to remember what everyone ordered. Have mercy on your server; ask for that separate bill.

Getting your server's attention to ask for the bill will vary. In a fancy restaurant, you can't yell and wave your arm—but you can raise your hand and beckon for them that you want the bill. Whereas in a bar, you can request the bill by either yelling or gesturing for it in sometimes questionable gestures. The number one rule of dining etiquette is to consider where you are and what might be acceptable or unacceptable behavior.

TABLE MANNERS

This is something a lot of people can skim over once and a while, especially the previously mentioned smackers—they are a special breed put on this Earth to torment unsuspecting souls.

The basics:

- Always pass the food from the left-hand side to the right-hand side—and ALWAYS ask for food to be passed, do not reach over the table.
- Pass the salt and pepper together so guests don't have to look for them if they're separated. Do this even when the guest only asks for one or the other.
- Never pass the desired item from one hand to the other. Always place them on the table.
- Don't snag food while the plates are in passing; instead, wait for your turn.
- Use the serving spoons to serve yourself, never your utensils. We don't want your saliva on the food.

SPECIFICS

- When dining in a formal or informal setting, or even at someone's house, some rules should be followed no matter where you dine.
- When sitting down to dine, remove the napkin from its setting and place it in your lap.
- When standing to excuse yourself from the table, lightly fold the napkin and place it next to your plate. DO NOT

use the napkin to wipe your face or utensils; never wipe your nose with it—that's just distasteful.

- After eating, place your folded napkin to the left of your plate.
- The dinner begins when the host starts to unfold their napkin.
- And the dinner ends when they place their napkin beside their place setting.
- Never belch or burp at the table or fart—but you should already know that.
- Do not stick your fingers in your mouth at the table.
- If you receive your food before the other guests, wait patiently until they've also received it before eating.
- Lean over your plate when taking a bite so the food falls onto the plate instead of falling into your lap.
- For the soup—scoop the contents moving in a direction from your body to the middle of the plate. Never scoop from the plate towards yourself.
- Don't slurp or make any disruptive eating noises.
- Don't slouch and put your elbows on the table.
- If your hair is long, brush it over your shoulder to prevent it from dragging through the food.
- The most important tip is to always be yourself. You are wonderful.

Next, let's talk about manners when dining and tipping out on the town.

WHEN TO TIP

Because it has become quite the topic recently, it can become confusing how much to tip and who to tip. The waiter, but how much is an acceptable amount without having to break the bank? Because let's be honest, when you're a student, the money isn't really "money-ing" as it should or as you want it to be.

Restaurant servers usually expect (I use the word lightly, as most of them don't expect anything) at least 10-20%, food delivery services at 10-15%, with bartenders only wanting a more affordable 5-10%. Baristas are looking at an even lower tip rate than bartenders, with a whopping 0-5% (a real bank breaker).

My best advice is to consider what the person serving you has been going through. For example, if you are a table of at least twelve people, each with their complicated order, you might consider tipping that 25% and then some. And to be honest, it's always good to do something good for someone else. That barista's 5% tip could have changed their life. You never know. The tipping rates for other services are as follows:

- Moving services are usually tipped in the margin of 5% to 10% of the cost overall. If it's a larger movement with bigger items, you're looking at 15% to 20%.
- Hotel staff—for valet, you're looking at $2 to $5 and $5 to $10 for the concierge.
- Massage or spa services are expected to get at least 15% to 20%.
- Housekeeping deserves a reasonable $2 to $5 tip per day, and I would argue that it is very much earned and deserved.
- Beauty services such as nails and hair are usually tipped between 10-20%.
- For Uber, you can tip 10-20%—adding at least $2 if they help you with your luggage.

Don't Forget to Tip

WHEN NOT TO TIP

The previous paragraph might have frightened you—because it can be a lot. Remember who expects how much and how to determine the correct tip amount from the overall price. And let's be honest. It seems like everyone expects a tip these days—some of them do not earn that tip. We've all experienced the rude waitress that does the bare minimum, and we've all encountered that rude employee that made it hard to tip into their hand or set it apart from the bill. Because it happens, and not everyone deserves that 20% they expect.

So I'm here to tell you that it is okay if you don't always have the means to tip or don't want to. Of course, it is ideal in the name of etiquette and being a good person, but it's not always necessary or fitting. Here are some instances where you don't have to tip:

- Professionals -People like doctors or physicians, psychiatrists, or even nurses never expect to be tipped— because it's unethical, and it would be weird, in all honesty. Just imagine, "Hey, doc. Thanks for patching me up. Here's an extra $20 to add to that steep medical bill. Just in case you need it."

- Skilled Professionals - Skilled Professionals such as plumbers or electricians don't get a tip because they work based on a contract and are compensated based on their work and hours. So they are being compensated to the full extent they deserve and have worked for, and they don't require a tip as servers do— who are paid minimum wage by the hour.

- When the Tip is Already Added - At some restaurants, a text on the slip will say if gratuity has already been added and how much. If there has already been a certain amount added to your total, you don't have to tip again.

- Small Businesses - You don't have to tip when ordering something from small businesses or utilizing their services since they already work their prices to include service, delivery, and production costs. Of course, some allow tipping, but you don't have to if you don't have the means or simply don't want to.

I GOT BILLS IN MY HANDS

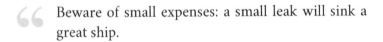 Beware of small expenses: a small leak will sink a great ship.

— BENJAMIN FRANKLIN

*M*oney, money, money. It really must be funny in a rich man's world. But to you and me, it's the source of a lot of stress and sometimes sadness. The latter is especially true if it's the main factor that's withholding you from doing something you love or achieving something you know you're able to, such as graduating college or even attending in the first place.

Financial literacy is a must for any college student these days because you have a "blank page" to start from—in other words, you don't have any debt or any financial crutches at this stage. You are able to create a good financial "plan" for yourself—so you best focus as we discuss it.

FINANCIAL LITERACY

The importance of financial literacy is not only because you'll better identify the good from the bad choices regarding your finances, but you'll also gain a deeper understanding of everything else under the umbrella of finances. For example, you'll be able to identify and sort your salary better, and you'll be able to juggle your financial obligations better.

You will be able to protect yourself from financial loss and understand the risk and rewards of investing and saving. You will be able to apply for loans and have a solid plan to pay them back. In other words, financial literacy is a secret weapon you can use to simplify your life immensely.

IMPROVE AND MAINTAIN YOUR CREDIT SCORE

As discussed in chapter one, your credit score is the amount of loans you have applied for and managed to pay off. The better your score, the more opportunities you will have—because you cannot rent an apartment, buy a car, etc., without it.

Your credit score depends on the following:

- Your payment habits and history. If you are able and have always paid your debts on time or within the set deadline.
- Your age.
- The amount you owe and if you have good habits of paying your debts.
- How much you make use of your credit. Do you use it for any old thing and neglect to pay the amount you owe back, or do you use it for emergencies and are reliable regarding payment?

IMPROVING YOUR CREDIT SCORE

If you feel like your credit score is too low or just want to improve it to take precautions for the future, you can focus on the steps below to make that happen.

KEEP AN EYE ON YOUR CREDIT REPORTS

Always review your credit reports to make sure you are immediately aware of any oddities caused by yourself or something else. Remember, you can only fix a mistake if you know it.

ALWAYS PAY ON TIME

Try to pay your debts on time and in full whenever possible because it saves you a heap of trouble later. This will reflect well on your payment habits, and you'll be more likely to receive a loan—should you need it one day.

CONSIDER USING AUTOMATIC PAYMENTS

Automatic payments are payments that are set up with a merchant or other service provider so you can pay bills or other recurring payments. These are usually used for bills that you know are going to reoccur each and every month. This could be used for utility bills, credit card bills, gym fees, car payments, rent payments, insurance payments, etc. This is a very convenient way to make sure you pay your bills on time.

Automatic payments are set up directly with the company that you are doing business with. You give the company your checking account or debit card information, and then you sign something giving the "authorization" to electronically withdraw money from your account and withdraw this money on a regular basis and at scheduled intervals. You have the ability to stop these payments at any time. Automatic payments are a great way to save time and keep from ever paying late fees, but you have to be organized with your money and plan ahead for these withdrawals.

DON'T USE YOUR CREDIT FOR EVERYTHING

While it might seem like a never-ending well of wealth, your credit should only be used when absolutely necessary. You should aim to keep your credit utilization to or below 30% (R. Lake, 2022). However, if you feel that you don't have that much self-restraint, you can ask your creditors to put a limit.

LIMIT YOUR APPLICATIONS

If you're going to apply for credit or a loan with every purchase you make, you're on the fast track to a poor credit score, without a doubt. Try to keep your applications for things that are absolutely necessary.

You should expect to see a change in your credit score depending on how much of a 'beating' it took. If you missed one payment, then you should rebuild it pretty quickly. But it will take longer if you have a habit of not paying.

BORROW MONEY WISELY

The act of borrowing money from someone, and asking in the first place, can be a very awkward and sometimes embarrassing thing to do. Not because the people you borrow from make it a big deal but because you feel that sense of shame alone. It doesn't feel good, and it doesn't do wonders for your confidence. And the situation of lending money to someone is even worse because you are not guaranteed to be paid back. But what if I told you there was a way to go about this situation that might make it more bearable?

BORROWING MONEY FROM FRIENDS AND FAMILY

This is a daunting task because it requires you to be honest with yourself and admit you need help, and then you have to be brave and ask for help from your closest family and friends— and this can be difficult because you don't always want to admit that things haven't been going too smoothly. But I'm here to tell you that it's okay to ask for help when it gets difficult, as long as you don't take advantage of the good people lending you the money.

EXPLAIN YOUR SITUATION

The first and best place to begin is by presenting your situation and explaining why you need the money. This will make the lender more open to the idea because they will understand the situation better. You can't expect them to help you if they don't know the situation—for all they know, you don't even need the money.

Explain to them why they should lend you the money and why you won't be the cause of their financial loss. They need to know the risk will have a reward. You can even put up collateral to sell your case even further. Collateral is something of value (an asset that you own) that you would give to the lender in case you don't pay back the money. For example, you might give them the title to your car as collateral until you pay the loan back. You would continue to drive the car, but they would keep the title. If you did not repay the loan, they could come and take the car as repayment for your unpaid loan.

MAKE A REPAYMENT ARRANGEMENT

This arrangement should suit both parties, especially the lending party, because they run the biggest risk. And make sure you keep to that arrangement because there is more at risk here than just the money—your relationship with this person could be at risk, too, especially if you aren't trustworthy. Be serious about the repayment and set a clear due date; this will show that you're serious about the loan repayment and strengthen your case further. Set up a step-by-step repayment plan with your friend or family member, and show them how you plan to repay them and what minimum you can afford a month.

HAVE A BACKUP TO SAVE YOUR OWN HIDE

There are many times that life gets complicated and over-whelming, and the best-made intentions have to be changed because of other, more emergent situations. There are times that these emergencies make paying back your loan in the agreed-upon time impossible. To reassure the lending party that you are willing to do whatever it takes to repay them, you can offer to pay the penalty or offer something for collateral should you fail to meet the due date. This decision has to be made only after you have looked at every available option because this will require your original loan to cost you a considerable amount more than you had initially planned.

HAVE A WRITTEN AGREEMENT

This is probably one of the best ways to reassure the person that you are serious about paying them back and that you desperately need the money. Ensure that both you and the other person get a copy and that both have signed—to solidify the agreement. This protects yourself and the other person and is a great reference material if arguments arise.

LENDING MONEY TO FRIENDS

The Do's

If you expect to get the money back from whom you lent it to, it would be wise to consider to who you lend the money. While you might think that friends and family are a safe bet, it's not always the case. Some of them might take your bond with them for granted and assume that you don't have to pay them back—and that's where it becomes fickle. The best way to prevent a financial loss is to:

- Only lend money to people you trust absolutely and with no doubt.
- Only lend an amount of money you can afford comfortably; you don't have to break your bank to help someone—you need to eat, too.
- Try to get the agreement in writing, not because you want to be mean-spirited, but because you want to protect yourself. Your loan "contract" should include the following information.
- Yours and the borrower's name.
- The amount of money.
- The date you loaned the money.
- When the loan should be repaid.
- Any consequences should the borrower try to weasel out of it.
- Always make sure to collect that payment—unless you are willing to give it away as opposed to lending someone the money.

The Don'ts

There are some precautions you need to take when it comes to lending money—because it can go very wrong; very quickly.

- Never lend an amount of money that you cannot afford comfortably.
- Do not lend someone money based on guilt—but rather because you want to help this person. Guilt is not a trustworthy emotion to work from when it comes to money or any decision-making, for that matter.
- Do not—under any circumstances—use your credit to loan someone money; that is just asking for trouble. Because if you didn't have the money to lend to them in the first place, then you won't have the money to pay it off—especially if they don't pay you back.

MAINTAINING SCHOLARSHIPS AND FINANCIAL AID

Very few in this world can afford to go to college or university without the help of financial aid—and those who can, are usually accompanied by grumpy parents who are blind-sided by the outrageous number they are expected to pay. Getting an education is expensive, and it's hard work—even more so if you add the stress of keeping track of tuition costs, financial aid, and scholarships.

Students who rely on financial aid and scholarships to pay their tuition are especially focused on graduating with good grades because they'll need a job ASAP to repay those loans. This is why it's a good idea to start focusing on how to maintain those financial aids to keep yourself out of financial "hot water."

FINANCIAL AIDS

This section will cover everything you need to know on the subject—how to apply, how it works, when it goes into effect, how you repay the loan, how to maintain it, etc. Every need-to-know piece of information you'll ever need on financial aid is right here. Consider it your goldmine of financial information.

HOW IT WORKS

Financial aid can be granted via different branches—federal and state agencies, high schools, colleges, corporations and foundations, and some private institutes that are set up with this intention in mind.

The amount you are loaned depends on the regulations of the agency you applied with, as well as any repayment agreements and guidelines or requirements they need to follow to be able to help you.

If your application with them is successful, then you will be awarded the loan if you accept the offer. If you reject their offer, you'll have to reapply or look for another aid that suits your wishes better.

APPLICATION INFORMATION

• First, you need to file a Free Application for Federal Student Aid (a.k.a FAFSA)—an application that state agencies and some schools use to decide if the student needs college aid. You can access this application through the U.S. Department of Education.

• The application deadline is October 1st for the following academic year or June 30th if you attend in the fall. This application has to be reapplied for every academic year.

• Private colleges use the College Scholarship Service Profile (CSS Profile) form to pinpoint how to section their own aids. This is a more detailed form than the FAFSA form and takes more time to fill out.

• You must pay $25 for your CSS profile and $16 each for additional reports (*F. Powell, E. Kerr, S. Wood. U.S News, 2022.*) There are exceptions to this rule—usually, families that earn less than 100K can fill out the forms for free.

DIFFERENT TYPES OF FINANCIAL AIDS

You can get financial aid based on two factors; whether you are in need of it or if you have the grades for it. In other words, need-based or merit-based. For the former, a family's ability to pay for college is considered and calculated, on which the decision to aid the student is based. The latter is usually awarded by institutions, private organizations, or colleges for a special ability—musical talents, art talents, sports talents, etc. They are not based on your need for financial aid.

You are able to apply for federal, state, or institutional aid—but will receive different offers as each institution makes use of its own procedures and guidelines to determine the aid that can be given.

FOR FEDERAL AID, THERE ARE THREE FUNDING OPTIONS:

• Federal grant—This funding option means that the money they pay for your college tuition does not have to be repaid. The most popular grant in this section is the Pell Grant, and the granting of this is based on your family's ability to contribute and is calculated by FAFSA.

• Federal student loans—These are loans with a fixed interest and are funded by the government. These interest rates are decided and set on July 1st of every academic year and will be honored throughout the "life" of the loan. The main avenue for this type of loan is the direct loan program that allows students to borrow up to 31K if they're dependent and 57K if they're independent.

• Work-study—This is a program that offers part-time jobs on campus to help students with the repayment of their loans. Not everyone qualifies for this program, and you have to qualify through FAFSA in order to be 'enrolled' in this program.

• While you are able to qualify for need-based aid, you can utilize your own skills and aim for merit-based aid as well—anything that helps.

DEADLINES

Every institute will have its own application deadlines, and it's important that you are aware of each of them—you don't want to miss a golden opportunity. Sure, you can apply for aid all year, but it's better to have a head start and apply when the funds have not yet depleted. The worst scenario would be you qualifying for a certain financial aid but being unable to get an offer because of lack of funds—because you applied too late. Familiarizing yourself with the due dates of these institutions is the first step in your application plan.

APPEALING FINANCIAL AID AWARDS

So you've received your offer, but it is not at all what you wanted, and you were hoping for more. You are more than welcome to appeal the offer, but you need to remember that it should be within reason and with a good reason as well. There has to be a real reason why the institution or school has to review or reconsider your financial aid, and not just because you felt you had been awarded more. Keep this in mind before you appeal.

Appeals are usually only accepted if the family has suffered a significant change in their household income to the extent that they are now in need of more than just the funds offered. And you are only eligible for this appeal if the change happened in the time between your application and when you received the offer. You'll be expected to submit a letter.

MAINTAIN YOUR ELIGIBILITY

Well done, you've received your financial aid, and you're over the moon with happiness, more than ready to start your college journey. But the hard work does not stop here because you have to work to remain eligible for financial aid. These eligibility requirements are usually based on your grades, behavior, and your habits—how frequently you attend or skip class, your test grades, etc.

Your requirements will be set up based on your FAFSA information and your financial situation. They will also consider when you enroll, what you'll be studying, and the SAP (Satisfactory Academic Progress) you reported.

Any changes to your circumstances or the situation of additional aid should be reported because this changes the nature of your financial aid. Here are the changes that are worth reporting:

- any additional aid for tuition assistance.
- change in living situation or financial situation
- withdrawal from the college or university, especially if it's prior to the first day

TAXES

I think my very first nightmare as an adult was about taxes—because, honestly, it's *a lot*. Taxes can be extremely confusing and challenging, especially if you know nothing about it, which is the majority of the population. So here's everything you need to know about taxes.

WHO HAS TO FILE TAXES?

Your requirement to file taxes depends on the amount of money you earn. There is a standard deduction amount that sets the margin of income eligible for taxes, and those with the income margin that is not eligible. You can use an IRS tool to determine if you need to pay taxes.

If you earn more than the standard deduction amount, you also need to see if your employer already deducts the tax from your pay slip or if you need to pay the tax yourself—just to ensure that you aren't losing more money than you need to. The same is to be done if you do not have to pay tax; if they have deducted the amount from your pay slip, then you need to enquire for a refund because it is money you didn't need to pay in the first place. However, you will have to file the tax return in order to get the refund. If you are required to file for taxes, then your guardians should not have your income reflected on their tax reports—as you are not dependent on them.

DOES MY JOB REQUIRE THAT I PAY TAXES?

Let's say you have a gardening or babysitting job, it pays well enough, but you are unsure whether you are required to pay taxes or not. And the answer is easy enough—if you earn more than $400 from your job(s), then you will be required to file a tax return and report (in detail) what you earn from your job(s). You are also able to receive tax returns for any expenses tied to your job, as well as claim tax when you use your own equipment to complete the job.

WHAT IS NET OR GROSS INCOME?

Your gross income is the amount you earned before the deduction of tax, whereas your net income is the amount you earned after the deduction of tax, FICA, and social security.

WHAT ARE TAX REFUNDS?

A tax refund is when the taxpayer is reimbursed for any extra fees paid during the financial year. This is possible by submitting tax returns—documents submitted to the IRS and used to calculate how much you are to be reimbursed or if there is nothing to be refunded and you actually owe them money. Another word for this is tax rebate. The tax returns require the following information:

- your name and birthday
- your ID number
- your account details to the tax preparation site that you use—like your username and password (TaxSlayer is an example of an online tax preparation company that has a great easy to use, sometimes free, platform to prepare your taxes)

- a W-2—which should be sent by your employer

UNDERSTANDING YOUR CREDIT CARD STATEMENT

There are a whole lot of words on a credit card statement and a whole lot of numbers—so you should probably know what to look for to be able to determine any irregularities and anything that might not look right. And it's just better to understand what's going on because then you'll know what's happening with your finances. Your statement will have different sections; I will tell you what each specifies.

- Account Info—This section will include your name and surname, billing address, account number, and billing cycle dates. The billing cycle dates are important because it helps to determine your interest.
- Account Summary—This includes the payment due date, your payments and credits (if you have been paying the amount off monthly or if there is still a payment to be made), your total balance (which reflects how much you owe), and your other fees.
- Purchases—This section reflects when you used your card, where you used it (the vendor's name), the category of purchase (groceries, etc.; this is determined by reading the vendor's MCC code—which every shop has), and the amount you spent.
- Payment Information—Your credit card balance (how much you owe to pay off the card balance), the amount due each month, the time it will take for you to pay the credit off, how much credit you have at your disposal, and the amount you have already paid.
- Account Details or Fine Print—This section includes your contact information, your rights as the cardholder, and a detailed breakdown of your interest rates.

- Interest Charges—This reflects your purchases, cash advances, and balance transfers.
- Rewards—Opening balance before this month, rewards earned this month, rewards redeemed this month, and amount able to be redeemed.

As long as you know how to read your credit card statement, you should be able to spot any irregularities easily and catch them before they get too out of hand.

RENTER'S INSURANCE

This is a very important section because it is something that is an absolute MUST in the adult world. It's important because it covers everything from stolen goods, injuries to your guests, bills, and so much more.

WHAT IS COVERED

Every piece of property in your home, from furniture to utensils, clothes to kitchenware, jewelry to electronics—renter's insurance covers all of it. Your insurance will give you an option for reparations or replacements if the item is damaged by something outside of your control—like natural disasters, theft, etc.

Additionally, your insurance also covers you for any injuries your guests sustain and any property damage to other people's belongings, for which you are able to legally be held liable.

Suppose you are unable to temporarily live in your home due to unforeseen circumstances like natural disasters. In that case, etc., you can claim additional living expenses to cover your lodgings elsewhere while the problem is being resolved or handled. To be more specific, here is a list of things covered by renter's insurance:

- explosions
- aircrafts
- any falling objects
- hail, smoke, the weight of ice/snow/sleet
- theft and vandalism
- fire or lightning, as well as freezing
- riot and sudden damage due to burning, cracking, bulging, tearing, or short-circuiting
- volcanic eruption
- storms—where damage was sustained

COVERAGE AMOUNT

This is where you'll need to determine the amount of insurance you'll need based on the amount of property (and its value) you have. This is what you'll call your home inventory, and it will contain the following:

- descriptions of all of the items you own
- the estimated value of each item
- the date it was purchased
- receipts and serial numbers (if possible)

If it's too difficult to make a list on paper, you can use the National Association of Insurance Commissioners home inventory app—ah, the wonderful world of technology. After entering your data, it will give you an estimate—although the normal estimated amount is usually between $20,000-$30,000, which can be increased if you need more.

CHOOSE A RENTER'S INSURANCE COMPANY

Choose a company by researching its rates, offers, and how much that will impact your monthly spending. If you want a starting point, you can look at your car insurance company—some of them offer joint accounts that help you qualify for discounts.

To make the decision easier, you can get quotes from different companies and compare their rates. This might help you to clarify the subject and which company would fit best with your financial capabilities and what you want in an insurance company. After choosing your company, you can choose an account you're interested in and apply online.

DEALING WITH UNEXPECTED EXPENSES

Sometimes life has a way of kicking you in the butt, especially regarding finances. There's always something to be paid for as soon as you feel like you've saved enough money. There's always something that wants to bleed your account dry. That's why you should make provisions for the unexpected, and the best way to do that is to start an emergency fund, take out a loan, or review your expenses.

EMERGENCY FUND

This is the life raft you'll be using when the tsunami of life comes to sweep you away—and drown you because life is cruel like that. An emergency fund is a good idea because it ensures you'll be able to pay for your necessities even though you might have unexpectedly had to give out more money than necessary —maybe for new car parts or to replace a household item.

Of course, you don't have to take huge chunks of your salary to make this emergency fund happen; a little goes a long way. As long as you're just doing what you can to help you in the future. They'll thank you.

TAKE OUT A LOAN

If you're in a tough place and haven't had enough time to set up your emergency fund, you could consider applying for a low-interest loan. Of course, you can only do that when you're absolutely certain you'll be able to pay it back in due time.

REVIEW YOUR EXPENSES

Each and every one of us have some area in our lives where we might be overspending—and in that area specifically, we are not open to making changes. But sometimes, it's necessary to reevaluate where our money's going, especially if it's hard-earned.

And if all else fails, you could always try the old-fashioned way and sell some of the junk you don't use anymore.

PAYING BILLS WITH AUTOMATIC PAYMENTS

Automatic bill payments are regularly occurring transfers to vendors frequented and set up by the account holder. They can be used to pay bills, electricity and water, subscriptions, etc. This is an especially useful tool if you're forgetful of payments because the money is automatically withdrawn from your account each month on the same day.

You can schedule these payments through the recipient's website or your banking app and link the payments with your debit or credit card—depending on which you use for your payments.

There are many benefits to this system:

- It saves time.

- You'll have a better credit score.
- Your payments will be made, meaning that you won't forget to pay anyone ever again.
- You have regular cash flow
- It's just easier and more efficient.

Have a System for Paying Bills

Whatever system you decide to use for paying your bills, it is critical to keep a detailed record of income and expenses. You have to know what you have coming in and what you have going out. If you decide to use automatic payments, they have to be at the top of this list because if there is not enough money for the automatic payment to process, penalties and consequences can be severe.

The next chapter is vital—and some would argue that it's the most important—part of growing up, and that is communication. Everything you say impacts making or breaking something in your life. There is a reason why everyone muses that communication is key.

Sharing Resources

"Connecting is one of the most important business—and life—skill sets you'll ever learn." – **Keith Ferrazzile.**

Statistics show that the average person comes in contact with 19-27 people every day and that twenty-year-old people usually come in contact with more than that. Every person we come in contact with is an opportunity to make a connection. These connections give us an opportunity to help and to be helped. As you make connections, I urge you always to put your best foot forward because you may be connecting with your next boss, CEO, preacher, spouse, or in-laws. With many of these connections, you have the opportunity to connect with and make an impression on someone who has the potential to really impact your life.

An old Chinese proverb (and quoted in Acts in the Bible) says, "It is more blessed to give than receive." The daily connections we make give us the opportunity to contribute to other people. You never know what that person is going through, and you have the opportunity to make a difference in their life.

My hope in writing this book is that I have been able to make some sort of connection with you, the reader. I hope that you can find 2-3 things in this book that can make a positive difference in your life. My goal is accomplished if I can help just one person.

You can help me reach my goal by helping me connect with a few more people.

By leaving a review of this book on Amazon, **you'll show new readers just how important these essential skills are and exactly where they can find the information they need to help them prepare for the future.**

Simply by letting other readers know how this book has helped you and what they'll find inside, you can help us connect with more people.

Thank you for your help with this. This age in your life is so important, don't waste another minute!

>>> Scan the QR code below or <u>click here</u> to leave your review on Amazon. Thanks again for your help. R. London

5

COMMUNICATION -THE GAME OF CONVEYANCE

> To effectively communicate, we must realize that we are all different in the way we perceive the world and use this understanding as a guide to our communication with others.

— TONY ROBBINS

*E*verything in life is about communication, and it's the only thing that keeps this nightmare of a society going. You must know how to communicate with people you're comfortable around and with people outside of your normal social circle. You need to be able to communicate with your peers and your superiors when you get a job, and especially with your clients—if you get a job that requires you to deal with clients/customers.

Communication is an essential life skill, one that can simplify your life or make it all the more difficult. For you, a student, it is even more essential because it helps you navigate college life easily—people who don't know how to communicate correctly risk falling behind in school, disconnecting from their peers, and withdrawing from society altogether. None of the previously mentioned is good for your mental health, either.

BENEFITS OF COMMUNICATION

Communication is the act of expressing yourself, your feelings, and your needs. It is done in verbal form and in text, email, body language, or physical expression via movements or hand signs. Regardless of how it is conveyed to the recipient, the core of communication is the ability to accurately express information to others in a concise manner that they easily understand.

Remember that communication is not necessarily what you say but how the recipient receives the message. Unfortunately, the interpretation of what you say can come across as entirely different than your true meaning. Now I know that there are many unreasonable people in this world, and you may think that you cannot be reasonable to someone misinterpreting what you say. Still, it will only benefit you by trying to ensure they receive your intended message.

VERBAL COMMUNICATION

When it comes to verbal communication, you need to be aware of the tone and articulation of your words as you convey the message to someone. Consider the information you are trying to communicate and how they would receive it best. For example, if it's about a sensitive subject regarding their relationship, you might want to consider your choice of words and how harshly you will inform them—for instance, "I'm sorry you guys broke up. But in all honesty, he/she was a real jerk." While this sentence might make you think it will make them feel better, it probably won't because they might still have some feelings for this person. Instead, try, "I'm so sorry you guys broke up. But maybe it was for the best; you guys weren't always kind to each other." Another option (and possibly the best option) is just the them that you are sorry they broke up and not add your opinion at all.

The same goes for other subjects like confronting someone on their behavior or the money they owe you. No matter the situation, you must remember that many unspoken words can be interpreted from your tone of voice, the context, and how you address the situation. Lack of proper articulation can lead to a lack of understanding in situations where it might make a huge difference.

NON-VERBAL COMMUNICATION

Non-verbal communication is most commonly referred to as body language—because it can speak just as loudly as words. You can convey many emotions like discomfort, excitement, stress, and so much more just with your body. For example, that person who's always biting their nails while in public? Chances are, they have serious social anxiety and could use a little help. That girl/guy that barely hugs you when you greet them? Chances are they don't really like the intimate act of hugging.

It's important to remember that your approachability is determined by the body language you put forth. You won't be approached as easily with your arms crossed and a frown deep as a crater on your face, but you might be approached if you relax your arms and drop the frown. Body language makes a huge difference if you know how to look for the signs.

LISTENING

A good communicator knows that half of it is not about speaking but about listening to others. Everyone's favorite subject is themself, and you will quickly connect with someone by letting them talk about themself. Communication is a two-way street, so you better be able to listen as well as you can dish it out. By being an active listener, you can internalize what is being said, improving your ability to interpret and respond better to the listener.

You don't become a better communicator by being the only one that does the talking but by being open to other perspectives and other methods of communication that might help you improve your ways. Think of listening as a crash course to improve your talking skills.

Always remember to be confident in yourself and your communication because it really does make a world of difference. Think about it; will you take advice from the guy that's too jittery to even finish a word without stuttering, or would you believe the guy who carries himself as if he's survived every life lesson he's been taught? Confidence is key, just as communication is key.

Effectively listening is a skill that is invaluable. Do not spend your "listening" time trying to come up with what you will say next. Instead, listen with concentration and focus. Don't try to listen to the big game while someone is trying to say something. Actively listen and focus on what they are saying.

COMMUNICATION IN EVERYDAY LIFE

The previous section was centered around communication regarding social settings and specific situations requiring careful consideration. But in this section, we'll tackle that social anxiety and talk about making appointments, leaving a voicemail, texting, emailing superiors, communicating with professors, learning to say no, and setting healthy boundaries.

EVERYTHING ABOUT PHONE CALLS

LEAVING A VOICEMAIL

Your voicemail should adhere to a certain structure, especially for professional business matters.

- Introduction—Something like, "Good day, this is Jon Snow," to which Ygritte can now respond, "You know nothing, Jon Snow," when she returns your call.
- The time and reason—State the time you are calling and the reason for your call, "It's nine in the morning, and I was just calling to find out if I truly know nothing."
- The request—Now, you request for them to call you back. "Would you please give me a callback at your convenience?"

- Rattle off your phone number for them to call, and then greet them before ending the voicemail.

Of course, if you are the one missing the calls, you'll need to have a voicemail in place for the callers.

- Start the same as before, with an introduction—"Hi there, you've reached Ygritte."
- Follow up—"I'm not available to answer your call at the moment."
- Remind them to leave their details—"Please leave your name and number, and I'll get back to you as soon as possible. Unless you're Jon Snow, then I don't want to know anything."
- End the voicemail—"Thanks for calling."

You can tweak the above with a few more professional words if it's for a business phone, but it's the same either way.

MAKING, CHANGING, OR CANCELING AN APPOINTMENT

MAKING AN APPOINTMENT

Making appointments can be difficult, especially if both parties are super busy. Therefore, you should try to make the appointment a while in advance, and the same goes for doctor's appointments. You can start the conversation with something like, "I'd like to make an appointment" for doctor's or dentist appointments, or "Are you free next Tuesday?" for more informal meetups.

The receptionist or your friend will give you an available date, to which you will then have to agree or disagree, and another suggestion should be made. From there, you'll agree on a date and a time, and then the appointment is "booked."

CHANGING OR CANCELING AN APPOINTMENT

If you have already made an appointment but forgot about a prior engagement, you must call and rearrange the date to match both parties again. When changing or canceling an appointment, always apologize and make these changes as early as possible to respect the other person's schedule. Just explain the situation, find another date that suits both of you and then the appointment will have changed. It's the same for a cancellation—just name the date and time of your appointment and why you need to cancel. Don't overshare the reason for the cancellation; the doctor does not care that your favorite ball game is more important than your annual earwax removal. If a conflict does arise, always reschedule the least urgent. For example, don't reschedule an urgent doctor's appointment because you have to take the dog to get a shampoo.

WHEN TO TEXT AND WHEN TO CALL

While texting may have taken over the world and improved some parts of communication, it has also hurt certain aspects of our communication. These days it's so easy to text someone instead of just talking to them—especially when it comes to the hard stuff like bailing on plans, breaking up with someone, or confronting someone. Texting can be bad for the following reasons:

- It promotes a lack of face-to-face communication—something that is already rare in today's society.
- It promotes bad behavior because you have your screen to hide behind instead of facing the consequences of your actions.
- Emojis can't always convey the exact emotions we're feeling—and they shouldn't have to because that's why we're able to express them in person.
- Face-to-face communication is better for those connections you're so eager to form, and it promotes a healthy relationship—because the screen isn't there to get in the way of your bonding.
- Many times texting can overcomplicate making plans. For example, complex meetings are difficult to schedule while texting because there are many details that have to be worked out beforehand. A phone call or in-person meeting can reduce the complexity of the plans.
- Texting has been the cause of many misunderstandings because you cannot hear the tone of voice the person is using. Therefore, assumptions can be made incorrectly, leading to a huge misunderstanding that isn't good for anyone.
- A phone call shows dedication and respect because you now give this person your undivided attention. And

there is nothing more lovely than having someone listen to you with full attentiveness.

- Texting is not as personal as you might think. And it certainly doesn't trump meeting in person or even doing the bare minimum and calling one another. Calling or meeting in person is much more intimate than texting, giving you the chance to build lasting relationships.

- Texts are too bland—in the sense that you can text anything and can't guarantee that anything is said with intention. You can't determine if it's also said with pure intention from your side and the other person's side.

Texting

In essence, texting isn't the best for any form of communication besides wanting to talk some gibberish with each other when you're not together. Any other form of communication, serious or not, should be had in person. It just establishes great relationships and lasting friendships that way—no great friendship was made via a text, just as Rome wasn't built in a day. That's not to say that all texts are bad. Texting can be a very efficient way to communicate. Below are some simple rules for texting that I like to employ.

RACHEL'S 8 RULES FOR TEXTING

1. Consider Who You are Texting – You need to address your preacher differently than your best friend.

2. Be Clear in Your Message – Text messages are notorious for being interpreted incorrectly. As we discussed earlier, the meaning of what you say does not always get received correctly. If there is any question about the clarity of your message, make a personal phone call. Remember, an emoji or an abbreviation can be easily misunderstood.

3. Respond in a Timely Manner – Unfortunately, the sender of the text assumes that you instantaneously receive their text, and they feel like you are ignoring them when you do not text back. That being said, you do not have to respond immediately, and this could even be rude or disrespectful if you are having a conversation, eating a meal, watching a movie, etc. If you cannot respond in 3-4 hours, a polite apology at the first of your test would be appropriate.

4. Be Mindful When You Send Emojis – Again, interpretation is paramount.

5. KISS (Keep It Short and Simple) – The goal of texting is efficiency. Don't be too wordy.

6. Always Introduce Yourself – Unless you are certain that the contact knows who you are, always tell them who you are. Do not assume that just because you texted them 2 years ago that they saved your contact information.

7. Use a Polite Greeting - A simple good morning, hope you are well today, or good afternoon are all good examples of a simple way to start the message.

8. Know When to End the Text – Be aware of when the person you are texting is ready to end the text. Certainly, do not badger them by asking, "Are you still there?" or "Are you ignoring me?".

EMAILING SUPERIORS

Sometimes emailing your superiors can be pretty straightforward, and sometimes it can be pretty difficult—if only for the lack of proper wording to describe a situation or ask a question. Email etiquette isn't really taught but is rather a skill picked up over the years. So here's a guide to help you should you have some second guesses.

- Always start your email with a respectful and professional greeting like "Dear" or "Good day." Your email should never start with an informal greeting like "Hey" or "What's up?"
- After your greeting, add the professional's or professor's name and surname with the appropriate contractions. For example, you can't address your superior with "Good day, Gordon Hollins." Some people might find it disrespectful, especially if it's your professor you're talking to. Rather opt for a "Good day, Mr. Hollins" and continue with the subject of your email.
- In the body of the email, provide some context to your situation by explaining what's going on and what you want some clarity on.
- Remember to specify which class you are in and which day you have class with this professor.
- Sign the email with your name, surname, and other contact details needed to reach you. Remember to keep it professional and not to sign off with something like "Cheers" or "See ya." Try for a more professional approach, like "Kind regards" or "Best wishes."

- If possible, please remember to send it from your university or college email and not your personal email.
- Always use full sentences and proper punctuation.
- Keep it short and to the point but detailed enough so that your professor will understand your situation.
- Keep an eye out for their response so that you can reply promptly.
- Never reply to a message before ensuring that it is going specifically to there person you think it is. Accidentally sending a message can result in embarrassment or worse if you copy the entire class or your ex when you thought you were replying to a professor.
- When asking for extensions, allowances, or exceptions, inform them of the situation first and how long you need the extension to be.

You've Got Mail

COMMUNICATING RESPECTFULLY

Communicating with your professors can be sort of nerve-wracking—because they aren't always the most approachable. Add to the mix your desire for inevitable disagreement about something, and it can be uncomfortable if you don't know how to communicate respectfully. The way to a teacher's heart is by showing them that you respect what they do for you, value their time, and appreciate that they are trying to help you build a future.

Sure, sometimes it can be hard because some professors might not like you, and you might not like them. But you'll be fine if you maintain a boundary and remain respectful. Here are some tips for talking to your teachers:

- Make an appointment with them first. They do have a life outside of teaching, and it helps to have the conversation in a professional setting. Catching up to them outside of class isn't always the best time for a talk.
- Plan what you want to say so that your information is carried over to them correctly and they can understand what you want to discuss.
- Make notes before the meeting on the specific topic you need to ask about or requests that you intend to make. Do not expect to just "wing it."
- If you're struggling with some of the assignments they gave you, don't use negative statements like, "It's boring" or "I don't really like doing that specific assignment." Instead, try to get their advice on how to tackle the assignment or simplify the problem to better understand it.
- While you can ask for their advice, you cannot expect them to solve your problems. Be a problem solver by suggesting solutions and asking them if they think this might help.
- Listen up—as in, really listen. You can't ask for your teacher's help but don't want to listen to what they have to say. That defeats the purpose of asking for help in the first place.

- Never assume your professor doesn't like you until they've said they don't like you. This will only cause a disconnect between you and your teacher and complicate your ability to ask them if you're struggling.

LEARNING HOW TO SAY NO

Saying no and laying down that boundary is a tough task for many people because it almost always has negative consequences. And it has a consequence because some people struggle with respecting boundaries and lash out due to their inability to comprehend healthy communication.

Firstly, it's important to know that you don't have to feel guilty for saying no to anything you don't want to do or want to be a part of. And while it may be difficult, it is also a very good way to set some healthy boundaries and communicate to someone that you are not comfortable with what's happening or what the other person wants you to do/agree to. But before we get to the "how" of the subject, let's focus on the "why" of guilt.

WHY SAYING NO IS HARD

Usually, the cause of this overwhelming guilt comes from childhood. We are taught to be polite and patient, to let some things go for fear of disrespecting others. And while there is some truth to the above, this is also the contributing factor to some people's difficulty with setting and enforcing boundaries.

The inability to say no can also be the cause of a lot of communication problems. When you do not just say no from the beginning, the person you communicate with assumes you are on board with them.

Not being able to say no can be because you grew up with the idea that saying no was connected to negative feelings and consequences—a perfect example of this would be saying no to a parent or teacher and getting reprimanded for it.

Another cause of this might be a lack of self-assuredness and confidence—you doubt yourself and your reasons for saying no in the first place. In turn, you are sometimes unable to say no, because you feel a need to establish yourself as someone who can carry the weight of everything. Have self-confidence in a situation where you need to put your foot down and demand a change from someone.

If you are an empath, then your inability might stem more from the fear of disappointing or hurting someone rather than innate imposter syndrome or something from your childhood. Humans crave connection and socializing by nature; therefore, we want to do everything possible to keep those connections from severing. We crave a sense of belonging, of camaraderie, and that's why we're hesitant to do anything that might potentially ruin that sense of belonging or disappoint others.

WHEN SAYING NO IS TOTALLY OKAY

Saying no anytime you feel uncomfortable is okay, but if you need a little more guidance, you don't have to worry. Sure, it might be a little difficult at first, but once you listen to yourself, it will be as easy as breathing. Even though saying no is totally okay, be aware that saying no to a professor about a required assignment may have consequences (such as a lower grade or worse). This same thing applies to saying no to a boss about a job requirement, as this could result in you being bypassed for a job promotion (or loss of your job altogether).

WHEN YOU FEEL OBLIGATED OR GUILTY

When you're a freshman in college, some seniors may think they can delegate tasks to you because they're your superiors. The same goes for every other aspect of your life. If you feel like you're being taken advantage of because you're in an inferior position or because of your kindness, don't be scared to say the big NO.

IF YOU FEEL IT VIOLATES YOUR BOUNDARIES

If you feel like their request does not align with your boundaries and that they don't respect them, don't hesitate to shut it down immediately. You set the boundary for a reason, and you had the emotions to back that boundary for a reason—don't doubt yourself now.

IF YOU FEEL LIKE SAYING YES BECAUSE YOU WANT TO PLEASE THEM

This is the biggest no-no when it comes to communication and healthy relationships, for that matter. You need to feel safe enough to say no to this person without fearing that they will be upset or not like you anymore—because that's what's keeping you from saying no in the first place. You need to be able to tell this person no, without worrying about negative consequences. It is not your job to please everyone, but it is your job to protect yourself.

THE IMPORTANCE OF SAYING NO

You are able to live a much more fulfilling and high-quality life if you learn to say no because you will no longer be trapped in the commitments you made when you were unable to. You won't have to do anything you're uncomfortable with anymore. You will perform better in all areas of your life because your assertiveness grants you the freedom to pursue things that you find beneficial to your growth (in both your personal and professional life). You'll be able to focus on yourself instead of focusing on how you affected the other person.

Additionally, you will start building strong relationships built on trust and respect because they respect your boundaries. This, in turn, helps you respect yourself by achieving your own goals —because you're no longer caught in other people's stuff. Lastly, you will have much better mental health because you won't be stuck with guilt and second-guessing anymore. It sounds like a win-win situation to me.

TIPS FOR SAYING NO

Practice saying no on a daily basis. If it's daunting, start with small things like saying no to a barista for extra milk or sugar. It's a habit that needs to be introduced into your daily life.

- Communicate with the person why you said no, and why you decided to say no in the first place. If they understand where you're coming from, they might respond better.
- Take your time—if you have it—to consider your options and whether you want to say no. If you're uncertain, that's okay. Just take your time.
- Always be respectful with your words—saying no doesn't mean you have to be mean—but be assertive. There is a difference between the two; assertiveness is being unable to be swayed in your decision. Mean is just being mean and disrespectful.
- Don't be afraid to ask for advice when needed, especially when you're trying this "saying no" thing for the first time.

6

YOUR OWN MENTAL HEALTH ABOVE EVERYTHING

> There isn't anybody out there who doesn't have a mental health issue, whether it's depression, anxiety, or how to cope with relationships.......Just know that there is help, and your life could be better if you go and seek the help.

— HOWIE MANDEL

*M*ental health has become a hot topic recently—and for a good reason, because it wasn't talked about nearly enough in the years before. The things that happen in our lives leave bruises or imprints on our minds, like tiny reminders of everything we've endured and not resolved. Knowing how to take care of yourself and strengthen your mental health will benefit you, especially now as you enter adulthood.

Mental health can be defined as the absence of mental illness and the ability to react soundly and contemplate both mentally and emotionally. It is when you can approach issues with clarity, reduce the amount of stress you feel as a result of the issues, and solve problems efficiently.

Mental illness can be defined as the presence of psychological trauma and/or a psychological illness that influences your ability to act efficiently and without stress—and as a result, the person's moods and state of being are also greatly influenced and impacted. Medical conditions affect daily life and, sometimes, the ability to socialize.

Make Mental Health a Priority

EVERYTHING MENTAL HEALTH

WHY MENTAL HEALTH MATTERS

Prioritizing your mental health is always a good idea because your mind is the engine that keeps the machine of your body running—if it isn't working as it should, it can impact you greatly. Your mental health in college will serve as the foundation for the rest of your life because the struggles and the stress will only increase as you age and enter a working environment, start a family, etc. Your college experience is a once-in-a-life-

time experience—you will very seldom get the same opportunities as you will in college; therefore, your head has to be
squarely on your shoulders.

Sure, it's not always as easy as they say—which is why most
colleges and universities have great mental health centers to
help their students when they desperately need it. These centers
or programs consist of a network of professors, mental health
professionals, and some seniors who help you with all of the
burdens you're shouldering. There is more to mental health
than just being able to react properly and your ability to process
stress because your mental health can impact your experiences,
academic achievement, and well-being as you navigate college
life.

Many important life decisions occur during this stage of life,
such as lifetime friends, potential spouse selection, career estab-
lishment, work ethic, and many more. A solid foundation of
strong mental health is paramount to ground these decisions.

IMPROVING OR MAINTAINING MENTAL HEALTH

Besides seeing someone to help you recognize any negative
patterns or to help you cope with your mental struggles, you
need to know how to take care of your mind by yourself as well.
Your mind is a tool that needs to be honed and taken care of,
especially if you suffer from mental illness.

MAKE A MENTAL HEALTH GUIDE

I don't mean to write a whole novel about it (the irony is not
lost on me), but at least compile a list of resources to use if you
start feeling that pressing feeling again. Make a list of wellness
centers around campus, a number you can call if you need
serious help, make a note around your primary wellness profes-

sional, and especially make a list of some wellness apps you have used or want to use that might potentially help. Remember, you can only get better if you make an effort to—your mental health is your priority and responsibility.

EAT CORRECTLY

There is a reason why the phrase "You are what you eat" is popular. Some people try to joke and say that they can't buy mental health like a bagel in a coffee shop—a joke I particularly enjoy. But there is a lot of research that suggests that the foods you consume have an almost direct impact on how your mind functions. And think about it, if your mind is the engine, and your body is the machine—wouldn't you want to keep the machine running smoothly to lessen the strain on the engine? Wouldn't you want to keep all the parts oiled and clean so that it all can work together smoothly?

START EXERCISING

If you greatly despise exercise, you probably felt like chucking the book across the room at that heading. And I get it—I totally do, because exercise isn't for everybody. And some people even have a negative connotation to it because of some crazy personal trainers or fitness instructors that might have ruined that experience for them.

But there is more to exercising than just getting a rockin' summer body; it actually has to do with your brain. When you exercise, your brain releases chemicals called endorphins, which make the body and mind feel good—because they 'block' your pain receptors, making that mental anguish considerably less. This is why most people feel happier and more upbeat after working out or running. In fact, the National Health Institute, through a meta-study analysis, has shown that exercise is more beneficial for conditions such as anxiety and depression than standard psychotherapy or medications.

HAVE A STABLE SLEEP PATTERN

Sleep and maintaining healthy sleep patterns are essential for people who struggle with mental illness. Even missing three days of sleep can cause heightened anxiety, stress, and even depression. Set an alarm for the same time every morning, and go to bed at the same time each night.

SPEND TIME WITH YOUR FRIENDS

Have you ever had a good laugh with a friend and felt the weight of the world lift ever so slightly? Have you ever felt like drowning but then had your friends be the ones to throw the life raft? When we're with friends, our minds release feel-good hormones and make things seem less scary—especially so if you feel safe with this person.

ANXIETY

This can be defined as a constant feeling of uneasiness or nervousness, either in anticipation or fear of something bad happening. Anxiety can be worsened by external challenges that might force you to do something uncomfortable or participate in something outside of your comfort zone.

What makes anxiety such a crippling mental illness is that it triggers your fight or flight response, which causes your body to be in a state of hyper-vigilance almost permanently. Instead of being used when faced with real danger, it becomes a constant state of being. And while you might not be in actual danger, your mind still thinks you are because of your constant anxiety.

DEALING WITH ANXIETY

While it might not seem like it, there are ways that you can cope with overwhelming anxiety. Many people your age need a few methods to help them keep calm and keep their level-headedness as life starts to get a bit crazy. Here are some things to help get those feelings under control.

ADJUST YOUR MINDSET

Your mindset is the first thing that needs to be addressed if you want to change how your body regulates those feelings of panic —because that's where the source of the problem is. If you believe you are an anxious person and will forever be one, then you're setting yourself up for failure. You need to prepare your mind for the growth that's about to take place by moving from "it's about to" to "it's going to" happen.

BE AWARE OF HOW IT AFFECTS YOUR LIFE AND BODY

The next time you feel extremely anxious, take the time to notice how it affects your body and the way you perceive your surroundings. Do you have telltale signs of anxiety like sweaty hands, shaking, dry mouth, and rapidly beating heart? Well, those are the signs of your fight or flight being triggered. And while they can be uncomfortable, they don't necessarily result from immediate danger, and they can't do you any harm.

TAKE DEEP BREATHS

Breathing is the most effective way to lower your heart rate and settle your nerves. Breathe in for five counts, and then exhale for five counts. This aids your brain in the release of stress hormones that negatively impact your mental health by redirecting focus from your anxiousness to focusing on your breathing.

MEDITATION

Meditation and other relaxation techniques are usually very effective in battling the crippling symptoms of anxiety. They work because they help your mind redirect itself from the negative feelings that make your body react that way to positive thoughts and things that make you feel calm.

These techniques include breathing exercises, listening to calm music, yoga, etc.—basically anything that helps you to relax.

EXERCISE

As we discussed earlier, exercise has shown to be highly effective at combatting anxiety and depression. Through his meta-analysis study, Berman (2023) reported that Dr. Ru Singh showed that physical activity is 1.5 times more effective at reducing mild to moderate symptoms of depression, psychological stress, and anxiety than medication or cognitive behavioral therapy. And this exercise does not have to be racing up a steep mountain. The study went on to show that essentially all forms of exercise produced significant mental health benefits. So go for a brisk walk, a slow jog, and do air squats and push-ups, but get some exercise for your mental health.

SEEK PROFESSIONAL HELP

Some professionals can help you cope with the anxiety if the above-mentioned doesn't seem to help, and it's really impacting your ability to enjoy life and complete tasks. The medical professional will then determine if you are viable for medication or if there is a deeper problem that is surfacing in the form of anxiety.

The professional might also suggest cognitive-behavioral therapy—which is the act of identifying the thought patterns or beliefs that are causing your anxiety and how to either redirect or reduce those thoughts.

Another option that can be explored is biofeedback, which is not a usual method used, but it is the use of electronics to determine how your body reacts to stressful situations. This device measures your sweat, body temperature, breathing, heart rate, and so much more—using this data, the professional is able to choose the best form of treatment.

COPING WITH LONELINESS

It's totally expected to go through a rut of loneliness when you get to college, especially at that age. You're going through so many changes, both in your environment and within yourself— it's kind of hard not to feel lonely. You feel like nothing's really as it was, and you're unsure if you'll still have the people in your life you once had. I'm here to tell you that if they're real friends, you will still have them; you just might not see them as often as you had, especially if you're going to different colleges. Additionally, sometimes loneliness is just the thing you need to be able to find yourself, and you might find that it has a kind of solidarity that cannot be found in your friends and family— however great they are.

I want you to feel reassured that everyone feels lonely from time to time and that it doesn't mean that there's anything wrong with you. And while it may suck, it is a part of growing up. You are meant to experience new things, and you are meant to break free from all you've ever known—because you are meant to grow and meet new people who will add even more to your life. Think of loneliness not as an indication that you have no one because that's not true. Instead, think of it as a key that unlocks the room where your new friends and your new experiences are waiting eagerly to meet you.

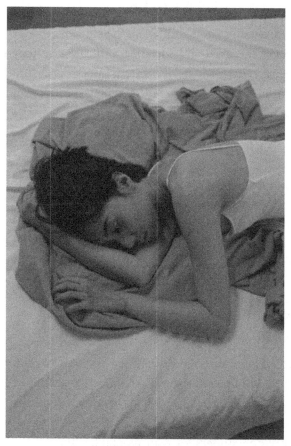

Loneliness

HOW TO BATTLE LONELINESS

If the loneliness stems from your fear of not having any friends or from not being able to make new ones—then there are some things you can do to fix that. All it's gonna take is your willingness to put yourself out there and some self-confidence.

VOLUNTEER OR JOIN A CLUB

Colleges are really good at offering the students many opportunities to get involved and socialize a bit because they have so many clubs, events, sports events, volunteer opportunities, etc., where the students are gathered in a neutral setting and able to converse freely.

Volunteering or joining a club is a golden opportunity to get out there and start making some new connections that have mutual and common interests in a certain subject. On the other hand, you might join a club that you know nothing about but just want something different in your life. College is a great time to explore new things that might interest you and volunteering or joining a club is a great way to see if you like these things.

RECONNECT OR STRENGTHEN EXISTING CONNECTIONS

If you feel a large disconnect between you and your friends, it's probably a sign that it's time to reconnect. You might be having this lonely feeling because you miss their friendship, or you miss their conversation, or you miss them. Reconnecting with friends can do wonders for your mental health.

INDULGE IN YOUR HOBBIES

Sometimes our loneliness can manifest as a result of something that we feel is absent in our lives. Do you have a hobby that you haven't been able to indulge in lately? Is there something you used to do that brought you joy, but you stopped suddenly after coming to college? Try making time for the things you love to do because that might very well be why you feel that gaping hole of loneliness. These things bring you joy for a reason, and it's a form of self-care if you indulge in them regularly.

DO A DEEP DIVE

The best way to battle loneliness is to figure out why you feel like this in the first place. You can't treat a cut if you don't know where it is, right? So do a deep dive within yourself, your feelings, and your mind. Talking to a counselor can many times facilitate this deep dive into your emotions. Try to determine when you started to feel like this and what you might suspect caused this feeling to creep up on you. From there, you can decide where to start beating this feeling and overcoming this barrier.

I want you to know that it might suck to feel this way because it really does. But it is only temporary, and you are great enough to make some wonderful new friends. This will not last forever.

BE YOUR OWN HERO

Everyone wants to know that there is someone out there that will stick by them and stick up for them, no matter what. It's only natural to desire that sort of loyalty and devotion, and it's especially beautiful if you have already managed to find it.

But if you haven't, you don't need to fuss—because you can be that person for yourself. Nobody will look out for you like you will look out for yourself. You have the power to stick up for yourself and to be your own advocate when no one else will. And you owe that to yourself because you deserve the kind of protection and support only you can give. You deserve to have people listen to your story and the value you add to their life. However, it's easier said than done, and if you feel like you can't do it, then here are some tips.

ACCEPT WHO YOU ARE

This is the part where you do some soul-searching to get to know yourself or to accept who you are. Self-reflection isn't always the easiest, I know, but it is the first starting point to really knowing who you are. That includes accepting your weaknesses as you have accepted your strengths, accepting your flaws as you have accepted your perfections, and accepting the darker parts of yourself as you have accepted the lighter parts of yourself.

With self-reflection comes the stark reality that while you cannot change who you are at the core, you can learn to embrace who you are and love yourself for it. Knowing your shortcomings is a strength not many have because they shy away from the truth glaring at them in the mirror daily. Realizing who you are is something that will empower you to be the best advocate for yourself. This can be difficult, but be honest with yourself when doing self-reflection. When you examine yourself at your core, sometimes you see a selfish brat. If this is the case, you have to fight this and work towards overcoming this selfishness because this will drag you down in the long run.

DEMAND YOUR SPACE

I don't mean in the self-entitled sense, but rather in the sense of claiming a space that is rightfully yours—in your personal life and in college. You won't get what you want and have people listen to you by politely asking for a turn to speak when they're ready to hear you out. You have just as much right as anyone else to be able to speak up for yourself, so demand that space and do it. You are allowed to be proud of who you are and all that you have achieved, and you are more than entitled to celebrate those wins as well. Selling or advocating for yourself is about more than just being able to take some heat. It's about being able to show your worth and making people realize the value you add to their life.

BE CONFIDENT

When it comes to the business world and even some situations in college, first impressions matter. By advocating for yourself, you are able to control the narrative someone will have of you—you will be able to control their first impression of you by selling your best points and being confident that you know what you're doing. If you believe you're capable of what you say you are, then they will believe it too. Fake it 'till you make it, as they say.

ACTIONS SPEAK LOUDER THAN WORDS

So you talked, but now it's time to walk the walk. It doesn't help anyone if you talk about a bigger game than you can back up, and you will have to pull through on that eventually. People like to see that you are able to deliver on what you have promised or guaranteed them that you can. Your actions have to reflect what your words say.

Nobody has got your back like you do, just like nobody will believe in you as you will believe in yourself. Be confident in yourself, even the darkest parts of you, and don't hide it away to ease someone else's discomfort. Demand the space, and show them why you belong there.

PEER PRESSURE

Don't even try to tell me that you are the only person in the world that doesn't buckle under peer pressure—not when you would willingly do anything your best friend tells you to do, even though it might not be the best idea. There's nothing wrong with it, though. It only becomes a problem when it affects your ability to complete tasks, achieve your goals, and set boundaries.

Peer Pressure

Peer pressure can be on both sides of the spectrum—it can be positive and push you to be a better version of yourself, or it can be negative and cause you to lose sight of who you are and what your priorities are. If you're struggling to identify some areas in your life where peer pressure might be at work, take a look at the small details. For example, feeling like you should act a certain way, getting involved in rebellious or dangerous acts, thinking you should dress a certain way, thinking you should react to something in a certain way, etc.

HOW TO BATTLE NEGATIVE PEER PRESSURE

SIMPLY SAY NO

You are allowed to set firm boundaries and let your friends or peers know that you are not comfortable with the request they've made. And they should respect it, especially if you have a friendship that is built on respect. Additionally, you have to allow yourself to leave the situation if you aren't being granted the respect you want and if the pressure is increased by these friends. You should not feel obligated to do anything you don't want to, and taking your power back by saying no is the first step to breaking that cycle of peer pressure.

MAKE AN EXCUSE

If saying no feels like too much of an aggressive approach, you can try another route and spew some excuse to get them to leave you alone. Of course, it has to be convincing enough that they don't consider pressuring you anymore—maybe using something like a medical condition might dissuade them from pressuring you to do anything regarding consuming some questionable substances. College is the playground for bullies wanting to get you to join them in their bad decision-making. But you have to remember that the decision is still in your hands.

BE HONEST WITH YOURSELF

If you're in a situation where you're actively being pressured to do something, and you're unsure how you feel about it, be honest with yourself and check in with your morals. Would you usually agree to this type of thing? Would you do something like this of your own accord? Be honest with yourself when you're considering these factors and base your decision on them—how you decide to react will depend on both of the previously mentioned.

TAKE NOTICE

The signs of an unhealthy friendship dynamic will make themselves very clear; you just have to notice them long enough for the light bulb to go on. Unhealthy dynamics are the leading cause of unhealthy peer pressure because it is done with the wrong intentions. Don't get me wrong, if your friend is pressuring you to be the best you can be, there's absolutely no problem with this. But the issue is when it's bordering on malicious intent.

As soon as those unhealthy dynamics are apparent, it's better for you to leave the situation immediately. You wouldn't want to be surrounded by people who have ill will towards you anyway, so why stick around to be their source of entertainment?

You have to empower yourself to say no to negative peer pressure; otherwise, that change won't happen, and you'll be stuck in the same old cycle for who knows how long. The golden rule of friendships are; if they don't serve you and your purpose, and make you feel totally at ease and supported, they would look better on the curb than at your side.

KNOWING HOW TO WALK AWAY

As you go through life, you will start to notice that some things just aren't as they should be. Whether this is for relationships, friendships, professional ventures, or your career, it doesn't matter. If anything in your life doesn't add value to it or seem to fulfill the role it's supposed to, then it's a good indication that it's probably time to let go.

Realizing that this person or this opportunity is not meant for you is the first and the hardest step you'll have to take—because with it comes the realization that you'll have to take active steps to potentially remove this subject from your life. It's heartbreaking, and it's tough, but it's also necessary sometimes.

The biggest reason why everyone has trouble walking away from something is because of the words what if? It seems to echo louder every time you get closer to that final decision, trying to pull you back in when you know it's not the best idea. If you find yourself in this position often, here are some tips to help you identify when it's time to leave and how to simplify it.

CUT THE EMOTIONAL CONNECTION

As long as there are emotions involved with your decision-making and your plan to walk away from this, it's going to be tough. Because all of those positive and negative feelings you felt during it will keep haunting you and making you second guess what you know is the best choice. Therefore, you need to try and take all of the emotions out of it—because just as emotion makes us human, they can also make us unstable when we need to make difficult decisions. Removing all emotions will only help you to process the loss that much easier.

Cutting the Emotional Connection

READJUST YOUR PRIORITIES

Sometimes, our ability to walk away is influenced by our prioritization of this person/situation over our own well-being. You know those words that echo in your head like, But what if he/she needs me? Or, What if the company needs me?

Walking away doesn't necessarily mean that it's because of negative events; it can sometimes happen because we want to pursue other opportunities, which is where the conflict of priorities comes in. As soon as you prioritize your needs above the other parties', that's when you'll be able to walk away without having the gnawing doubt trail you.

WHEN STAYING HURTS MORE THAN LEAVING

When you are in no better emotional state while in the situation than out of it—if you experience a worse type of sadness in this situation than outside of it, you probably have your answer already. You need to recognize and respect your feelings because they're trying to tell you that something is not as it should be. There's a reason why we get upset or angry or scared because it's our body's way of saying, Excuse me, sir/ma'am, but something ain't right.

You don't want to be surrounded by negative emotions every day, so why subject yourself to them when you know walking away is the better option?

FINALLY WALKING AWAY

So we've discussed how you can identify the signs and how you can simplify walking away from something that doesn't serve you anymore. But now we'll discuss the actual act of removing yourself from a situation—for good. Because deciding to do it and actually doing it are two different things and two different difficulties. Not only will you now imagine life without this person or this opportunity, but you'll actually be making it a reality. No take-backs and nothing to fall back on if you change your mind.

FACE REALITY

Because our emotions and bias can so greatly influence our perspective, you will need to take a moment of careful consideration. Think of your emotions as a piece of wool being dragged over your eyes, and realization being the one thing that can remove it to reveal the world in a new light. Once you face the harsh reality of the situation and why you are struggling, then you can remove the obstacle and depart with a clear mind.

MAKE A DECISION

Gather the amount of information that you feel you need, and consider each and every consequence of the decision you want to make. Weigh them against one another, and decide whether you want to continue with your departure or if you don't want to. Forget about trying to make a good decision because a good decision makes you happy and fits your desired consequence. Decide what you want based on your needs and what you want to see come out of this decision—and after you've decided, stick to that decision.

TRIGGER YOURSELF

If all else fails, you can do what everybody else does (look at that perfect example of peer pressure) and try to trigger yourself into action. I will admit that I have had to use this method more than a few times to get myself to make that hard decision, do that daunting task, and spur myself into action.

If it's anger that helps you, then focus on the negative emotions this experience has brought out in you. Being triggered makes the devastation of removing yourself from a situation easier to bear—because then you feel like you haven't really lost anything. But let's be honest, if you're considering this option, you've already decided to leave and just don't have the courage to do it. You got this, you are able to walk away, and you are allowed to walk away. Be like Nike; just do it.

MANAGING YOUR SOCIAL MEDIA PRESENCE

Always remember two things; one, there is such a thing as a digital footprint—so keep those toes clean—two, the internet is forever—so why don't we keep those private photo's exactly that; private. What you put on social media will always come back to haunt you because even though you erase it and you delete everything you don't want anyone to see, there will still be evidence of it floating around somewhere.

The fickle thing about it is that social media is no longer dismissed as something private and outside of work-related issues—you can now be laid off or seriously reprimanded for the things you put on social media, especially by your job and your college. There have been many times when people have gotten into trouble and lost life-changing opportunities because of the things they posted on their social media. Some argue it's justice, and others argue it should be completely separated from work. Regardless of your thoughts, it's a good idea to train yourself to manage your social media presence.

Managing Social Media can be Tricky

Additionally, if you want to increase your following and start an aesthetically pleasing social media presence—like all those influencers, you can use the tips below to achieve just that.

INCREASE YOUR SOCIAL MEDIA PRESENCE

CATER TO YOUR AUDIENCE

Think of your social media as a brand. With every video you post, you are selling yourself and your content to your followers (a.k.a. your consumers). Think of it as reminding them why they followed you and enjoyed your content in the first place.

Try to think of new ways that you can connect with your followers and how you can include them in some of the decisions you make. For example, host a poll for them to determine your next hobby or what you'll wear when you go out. Try to include them in your life so that they feel seen.

KEEP IT CONSISTENT

Once you've established a certain content creation schedule, you must be consistent with it. You can't post every day for a whole month and then fall into a rut and post once every 6 months; you won't be able to build a presence that way. Your followers will start to forget about you, and your relevance will disappear. Keep a consistent schedule, one that you are able to realistically maintain.

PATIENCE IS KEY

The thing about content creation is that you won't be able to build that vast following just overnight—it will require work and patience. Sure, you could make it easy and just buy your followers and views—but that's like boasting about an achievement that someone else did the work for. Take your time, create quality content, and be patient.

STICK TO YOUR VISION

If you have a certain vision about how you want your brand to be portrayed and viewed, then stick to it no matter what. Content creation is about authenticity and self-promoting your brand—it's pretty hard to commit to a brand that keeps changing its image, no? Therefore, decide what you want your brand to embody and stick to it.

7

THE PROFESSIONALS HAVE ARRIVED

> The way to get started is to quit talking and begin doing.
>
> — WALT DISNEY

As you finish your degree in college, your priorities and visions for the future shift. You are not worried about your next meet-up with friends or your next campus event— you will now start worrying about jobs, finding a place to stay, making rent, paying your bills, etc. As you get older and you approach the pivotal moment in your life where you move from young adult to adult, your mind will also shift and help you realize the importance of what's ahead. To help you with that change and to help you determine where to start, I've compiled a set of skills you will need to navigate the twists and turns coming your way.

FINDING A PROFESSIONAL

In college, you will need a lot of guidance, not only in your personal life or with your own ambitions but especially with your academics. That's why colleges and universities have such vast programs where you can find suitable mentors, tutors, wellness coaches, and so much more. They are there to help you through these changes and offer guidance and advice where they can.

Who you pick to help you with any area of your life will depend solely on what you're looking for in a mentor/mental wellness professional/tutor. If you want a semi-hands-off mentor that will help you navigate these trials without trying to steer you away from making your own mistakes and learning from them, you should probably steer away from an overly controlling person. The same goes for tutors; if you want someone to show you the basics and help you correct some things, then try to avoid the tutor trying to shove a whole textbook's worth of information into your mind in one sitting. What you choose will depend on your needs.

But how do you go about actually finding this professional? Well, there should be an information center on campus where tutors usually pin flyers of their services—and some of them are actually recommended by the information center as well. Regarding finding a mentor, well that will depend on your major and what you want to pursue—it doesn't help you at all to have a bio professor mentor you when you're in law, does it?

Additionally, you can find flyers of different tutoring services all over campus and on the online student portals—if your college/university has one. You can also hop down to the library and ask for a librarian to help you either find some helpful study material or make use of assistance to help you find some online study material that might be helpful.

There are many subject-focused centers on campus, from writing to math, from English to a student academic success center. You simply have to locate them and ask for assistance locating exactly what you're looking for—don't feel silly for needing help either; you're actually way ahead of the game because you asked for help.

FIND OR FORM A STUDY GROUP

What makes study groups such an efficient way of studying is that:

- You get to socialize while getting your work done.
- You are able to ask someone for help should you be struggling.
- You have someone to motivate you when the hours get long, and you are able to motivate them as well.
- You're not alone!

Study Groups

A successful study group is made up of a collection of people who are equally determined to focus and are willing to commit to a few hours of nothing but studying. You can look at inviting three or more people (these groups usually have five members) and invite them to a neutral location where you'll be able to focus and really get some work done without distractions.

When going to or hosting a study group, make sure you are going prepared—with your notes, textbooks, and all study material needed to have a productive study session. Your friends will likely need their own study material, so you can't count on borrowing theirs. Bring any and all notes about the subjects or topics you're struggling with so that they can help you efficiently. You can't solve a problem if you don't know what it is in the first place. Organize your work into sections, from most important to least important—or, you can organize them from what you know best and what you know least about; that's probably the most effective way.

Be efficient with your time in these valuable study groups. The best use of time occurs when phones are out of sight and silenced. Do not continually look at them to keep up with online life during this time with your study group.

APPLY FOR JOBS, INTERNSHIPS, AND ON-CAMPUS POSITIONS

GETTING A JOB

Ah, the lovely life of work. The bittersweet evolution of yourself from student to working professional—the great and anticipated change, if you will. Finding a job will seem like a daunting task at first—because you basically have nothing to show but a college degree and maybe some part-time jobs on your resume. And while they might not seem like much, they mean the world to an employer. And today, with everyone looking for experience instead of hiring a qualified candidate, you might feel like a tiny little goldfish in a pool full of sharks. It's totally normal if you do—because everyone experiences that deer-in-headlights feeling when they're first trying to put themselves out in the working world.

But where do you begin? Do you start with a resume? Do you start finding jobs, applying, and then setting up a suitable resume? What can you expect to happen during the process? What are they looking for? These are questions that haunt everyone, and why you should read this section carefully—not that it's that difficult, it's actually quite simple.

WHAT IS AN APPLICATION?

When filling out a job application, you will be required to offer information about your educational background, experiences and previous jobs, and the personal details needed to contact you for a follow-up interview. Recruiters and employers will use this information to determine if you are a fitting person to fill this role, and the extensiveness of the form will depend on what the company feels they need to know. These forms are usually found on job-hunting websites like LinkedIn and Indeed or the company's website. Please remember that you should attach your resume, references, and a cover letter to the application form.

APPLYING FOR A JOB

FIND JOBS IN YOUR DESIRED FIELD

The first step in your job hunting is to search for jobs that fit your desired field and pertain to what you studied. You can utilize websites like Indeed and LinkedIn to help you connect with employers more easily and to find a job suitable to your tastes without having to kill yourself looking for it. You are allowed to apply for multiple jobs and roles at once, and it's actually the smartest thing to do to ensure you have a backup plan if one falls through.

Don't forget to communicate and make connections. You might be surprised at how many times people want to help young people, especially those looking for jobs. See if you can find someone that you know or someone who knows an acquaintance of yours that works in the field that you are interested in. Ask them if you can chat with them, outside of work, about what to expect in this field and if they know of any available positions. Even if they don't know of any availabilities at the current time, you may have just planted a seed if something becomes available in the future.

Job Search 101

LOOK FOR OPENINGS

If you have had your eye on a certain company, you can keep an eye on their website to spot any openings that might be coming. This will help you determine if this is the work environment you want to be in and if this truly is the company you want to work for. Many companies also have social media pages that you can follow for updates.

SET UP YOUR RESUME

You need to update your resume because you'll be required to hand it in with your application, and it's essential that you have the correct information on there—you don't want to have to kick yourself about a piece of misinformation that cost you a job, do you? A resume should include your skills, recent education, certifications, and experience. Most of us dislike bragging about ourselves, but this is your time to shine and tell people about yourself. On your resume, do not hesitate to list your awards, achievements, and areas you excel in. If you do not tell them through your resume, there is no way for them to know these things. It is certainly acceptable to tell all the wonderful things that you have done, but do not lie. This can cost you an interview or even the entire job when the employer finds out that you lied. Honesty is undoubtedly the best policy.

APPLYING FOR AN INTERNSHIP

Internships are a great way to begin gaining experience in your chosen field without having to spend all hours of the day at the office—and it grants you the ability to study while working. Whether the internship is paid or not, you will still be "paid" for your service by the knowledge and experience you'll gain; there is always more to learn from the people and environment around you. Additionally, internships help you to gain a better understanding of the "world" you'll be stepping into once you've graduated, and it offers you the opportunity of working with other firms before you are fully immersed in the working world —helping you build a network of contacts before even really working full-time. Internships are a great way to immerse yourself in the field to ensure you want to do this for the rest of your life.

Internships are great in so many ways, but do not stop studying or ignore your assignments because of your internship. If you have assignments, put them first. Get them done promptly and on time during your internship times. This might mean that you have to work later into the night or get up earlier in the morning, but this hard work will pay off in the long run.

APPLY FOR THE TYPE OF INTERNSHIP YOU'RE LOOKING FOR

There are two types of internships: paid and unpaid in your respective career path. You now have to do the research to find out which of the two suits you best and which companies offer the best internship programs. Additionally, it also depends on what department you want to work in, and you should choose your internship placement based on that rather than where you think you'll have the most benefits regarding money, etc.

ASK FOR RECOMMENDATIONS

Getting recommendations from your superiors or the seniors in your college is always a good idea because they'll know the best spots to apply for great internships that will help you get a head start in your career. This is where the contacts you have made in clubs, organizations, and mentors you have worked with really come in handy.

UPDATE YOUR RESUME

Remember that your resume will be their first impression of you—so keep it professional and remember to list all of the information that could help you land this internship. Mention any skills that would be beneficial for a company to utilize, and try to have some references as well.

APPLYING FOR AN ON-CAMPUS JOB

These jobs are probably the best fit because your work hours are determined with classes in mind, and it's a great way to get into the habit of working while juggling other priorities. Not to mention that some campus jobs pay really well—though keep in mind that some don't pay at all.

DO SOME RESEARCH

The first step is to research open positions around campus and in some of the departments. You can cast a quick glance at the school's website to see if any vacancies have been listed, or you can contact the Human Resources Center and ask for some assistance.

EARLY APPLICATION

You know what they say, the early bird gets the worm. The earlier you apply for a job, the better your chances are of getting an interview and possibly getting hired. The best advice would be to apply before the new school season starts because if you apply after that, you run the risk of the positions already being filled.

Next, we are going to dive into a really boring but important topic......all the different forms of paperwork that you must know about.

8

WHY ALL THE PAPERWORK?

> Paperwork wouldn't be so bad if it weren't for all the paper. And the work.

— DARYNDA JONES

*G*rowing up requires many things besides partying and having fun. As we enter adulthood, we have certain responsibilities that we have to begin to take care of. Imagine for a minute that you are in a really bad accident and you are rushed to a local hospital. You are unconscious, and someone calls your parents; they rush to the hospital only to realize that they cannot get access to you or make decisions on your behalf because you are over eighteen and you have not given them permission to make decisions on your behalf. As adults, we need to be prepared, in advance of any medical emergency, by getting all the necessary paperwork in order to plan for the unexpected.

I recommend that you sit down with your parents, guardians, or someone that you trust and decide whom to name as your "agent" in the event of an emergency. Once you have that decided, then you need to make it official.

POWER OF ATTORNEY

This refers to a legal document you sign to grant another party the right to make decisions on your behalf—should you not be able to do so at one stage. They are referred to as a proxy or agent. The different types include:

- General Power of Attorney
- Financial Power of Attorney
- Durable Power of Attorney
- Non-durable Power of Attorney
- Springing Power of Attorney
- Medical Power of Attorney

It's important to remember that this person has full control to make decisions about you, your finances, your medical health, and your family when granted a POA. So make sure to choose someone you trust wholeheartedly.

HOW TO GET A POA

NAME YOUR DESIRED AGENT

There are some things to consider when choosing your agent. Some choose their parents, some choose their spouses, and some choose their legal-aged children. Below are some considerations when deciding whom to choose as your Power of Attorney:

- Are you able to name multiple people or a sole agent?

- Do you trust in their ability to make reasonable and conscious decisions?
- Will they make decisions to serve your best interests?
- Are you able to trust this person with your life?
- Will this person be able to make the correct decisions even while under emotional stress?

MAKING THE POA OFFICIAL

An attorney will be able to help you with your requests and guide you through the process of starting a POA. Another option is looking up information on trusted websites such as the American Bar Association. If you decide to use a physical attorney, probate lawyers are considered the best in this area. Probate lawyers differ from other lawyers because they are solely focused on estate planning, probate law, and elder planning. They can offer advice and guidance, and they are able to help prepare the required documents.

Please keep in mind that this attorney will handle all your affairs regarding your POA, that you should choose someone who is focused on your needs and desires, especially someone who is empathetic. They will be handling a sensitive subject, so some tact is needed.

FINALIZE DOCUMENTS

After the documents have been drafted, it is time to sign them and give them any legal "weight." Without your signature, your name's agent has no ground to stand on. Finalize the documents and ask for copies of them as well.

HAND OUT COPIES

After the documents have been finalized, make sure to send the signed copies to all of the necessary parties—such as your physician and agents, as the agents will be needed to hand them out to all necessary organizations for the correct procedures to take place.

IMPORTANT FORMS (HIPAA, FERPA, ETC.)

When you visit a doctor's office, walk-in clinic, emergency room, etc. you will be required to sign multiple documents before you can be seen. These include HIPPA, a medical release, a privacy agreement, and a few other forms. I want to give you a quick summary of each of these, so you will have a general idea of what you are signing.

HIPAA

A HIPAA form is a document signed to give medical professionals, organizations, and providers permission to use any medical information for treatment, payments, and operations. It is essential that this document is filled out correctly and signed in order for any of the above to take place. This also allows the providers to disclose your health information to the person that you have assigned as your health care agent. Of particular importance is the fact that this does not have to be all-encompassing since you can stipulate that you do not want to disclose information about mental health, drugs, sex, or any other details that you might want to keep private.

PRIVACY AGREEMENT FORM

This form is to ensure the patient is aware of and has agreed to the privacy agreement and that they will not be denied when requesting a copy of said privacy agreement. The agreement states that the organization complies with HIPAA and that the patient has the right to request their medical records at any time..

MEDICAL RELEASE

The organization must first complete this form before being able to share any medical information with other parties that are not the patient, their lawyer, or their insurance company— and even then, it's only allowed to be shared if it's an absolute must.

PATIENT AUTHORIZATION

These forms are designed to attain the patient's basic information—like their insurance, how they want to be contacted, etc. Organizations are able to confirm the insurance using this form and any other information that might be needed.

CUSTODIAN AGREEMENT

This form is signed by the medical health professional when they are about to leave one organization for another and are required to take the patient's information with them. This is documentation to confirm that the responsibility and documentation of this patient's information lie with the new organization now.

BUSINESS ASSOCIATE AGREEMENT (BAA)

This form is to be signed by any external organization that receives and reviews, or processes your medical information. It can only be done if the organization possesses a HIPAA BAA with all of its business partners to ensure HIPAA compliance is in place. This form protects the patient's information by ensuring that it is kept confidential and on a need-to-know basis. This is not necessarily a form that you will be signing, but a form that your doctor's office will sign with any business that they might give potential information about your health care. These include but are not limited to:

- Medical billing services
- IT service providers
- Accountants
- Practice management companies
- EHR cloud organizations
- Accountants and attorneys
- Shredding services

HEALTH PLAN COVERAGE

This allows the organization to store the patient's information and compile a record of their insurance and financial information. These forms are usually included in their policies to ensure that the insurance covers and the patient attends their appointments.

Now let's move on to an important form that you will need to fill out with the college or educational institution you may be attending, FERPA.

FERPA

These forms allow the student to share their educational records and information with external parties that might use the information. This can be their parents, colleges, universities, etc. To access this form, you'll have to use the Common App and complete the form. You may have used this app to apply to college. The Common App is an app that allows you to apply to most colleges in the United States and worldwide. It also allows you to send official transcripts to potential employers and other schools. From there, you'll navigate to "My colleges," select the school and then navigate to "Recommenders" or "FERPA."

In the "FERPA" section, you will click FERPA Release Authorization and then Complete Release Authorization to begin the process.

After completing the "Common App" form, you will have to navigate to "Naviance" and do your recommendation letters from there.

In "Naviance " you can click on your Colleges I'm Applying to and sync your accounts by using the same email, birthdate, and information—click Match if you're done.

Now that we are out of ink from all the paperwork, let's go find a doctor.